# ClearRevise

## Edexcel GCSE
## Business 1BS0

Illustrated revision and practice

**Published by**
PG Online Limited
The Old Coach House
35 Main Road
Tolpuddle
Dorset
DT2 7EW
United Kingdom

sales@pgonline.co.uk
www.pgonline.co.uk
www.clearrevise.com
**2020**

PG ONLINE

# PREFACE

Absolute clarity! That's the aim.

This is everything you need to ace the examined component in this course and beam with pride. Each topic is laid out in a beautifully illustrated format that is clear, approachable and as concise and simple as possible.

Each section of the specification is clearly indicated to help you cross-reference your revision. The checklist on the contents pages will help you keep track of what you have already worked through and what's left before the big day.

We have included worked exam-style questions with answers for almost every topic. This helps you understand where marks are coming from and to see the theory at work for yourself in an exam situation. There is also a set of exam-style questions at the end of each section for you to practise writing answers for. You can check your answers against those given at the end of the book.

# LEVELS OF LEARNING

Based on the degree to which you are able to truly understand a new topic, we recommend that you work in stages. Start by reading a short explanation of something, then try and recall what you've just read. This has limited effect if you stop there but it aids the next stage. Question everything. Write down your own summary and then complete and mark a related exam-style question. Cover up the answers if necessary but learn from them once you've seen them. Lastly, teach someone else. Explain the topic in a way that they can understand. Have a go at the different practice questions – they offer an insight into how and where marks are awarded.

# ACKNOWLEDGEMENTS

**The questions in the ClearRevise textbook are the sole responsibility of the authors and have neither been provided nor approved by the examination board.**

Every effort has been made to trace and acknowledge ownership of copyright. The publishers will be happy to make any future amendments with copyright owners that it has not been possible to contact. The publisher would like to thank the following companies and individuals:

Design and artwork: Jessica Webb / PG Online Ltd
Examination structure © Pearson Education Ltd
M&S store © Tupungato / Shutterstock
Toyota Factory © Lerner Vadim / Shutterstock

Graphics / images: © Shutterstock
Waveney House Hotel © SN Thomas Photography / Shutterstock
ASOS homepage © Casimiro PT / Shutterstock
Wagamama restaurant © Jeffrey Banks / Shutterstock

With thanks to GrantTree Ltd and the Waveney House Hotel for their case studies

First edition 2020. 10 9 8 7 6 5 4 3
A catalogue entry for this book is available from the British Library
ISBN: 978-1-910523-29-2
Contributor: Paul Clark
Copyright © PG Online 2020
All rights reserved

# THE SCIENCE OF REVISION

## Illustrations and words

Research has shown that revising with words and pictures doubles the quality of responses by students.[1] This is known as 'dual-coding' because it provides two ways of fetching the information from our brain. The improvement in responses is particularly apparent in students when asked to apply their knowledge to different problems. Recall, application and judgement are all specifically and carefully assessed in public examination questions.

## Retrieval of information

Retrieval practice encourages students to come up with answers to questions.[2] The closer the question is to one you might see in a real examination, the better. Also, the closer the environment in which a student revises is to the 'examination environment', the better. Students who had a test 2–7 days away did 30% better using retrieval practice than students who simply read, or repeatedly reread material. Students who were expected to teach the content to someone else after their revision period did better still.[3] What was found to be most interesting in other studies is that students using retrieval methods and testing for revision were also more resilient to the introduction of stress.[4]

## Ebbinghaus' forgetting curve and spaced learning

Ebbinghaus' 140-year-old study examined the rate in which we forget things over time. The findings still hold power. However, the act of forgetting things and relearning them is what cements things into the brain.[5] Spacing out revision is more effective than cramming – we know that, but students should also know that the space between revisiting material should vary depending on how far away the examination is. A cyclical approach is required. An examination 12 months away necessitates revisiting covered material about once a month. A test in 30 days should have topics revisited every 3 days – intervals of roughly a tenth of the time available.[6]

## Summary

Students: the more tests and past questions you do, in an environment as close to examination conditions as possible, the better you are likely to perform on the day. If you prefer to listen to music while you revise, tunes without lyrics will be far less detrimental to your memory and retention. Silence is most effective.[5] If you choose to study with friends, choose carefully – effort is contagious.[7]

1.  Mayer, R. E., & Anderson, R. B. (1991). Animations need narrations: An experimental test of dual-coding hypothesis. *Journal of Education Psychology*, (83)4, 484–490.

2.  Roediger III, H. L., & Karpicke, J.D. (2006). Test-enhanced learning: Taking memory tests improves long-term retention. *Psychological Science*, 17(3), 249–255.

3.  Nestojko, J., Bui, D., Kornell, N. & Bjork, E. (2014). Expecting to teach enhances learning and organisation of knowledge in free recall of text passages. *Memory and Cognition*, 42(7), 1038–1048.

4.  Smith, A. M., Floerke, V. A., & Thomas, A. K. (2016) Retrieval practice protects memory against acute stress. *Science*, 354(6315), 1046–1048.

5.  Perham, N., & Currie, H. (2014). Does listening to preferred music improve comprehension performance? *Applied Cognitive Psychology*, 28(2), 279–284.

6.  Cepeda, N. J., Vul, E., Rohrer, D., Wixted, J. T. & Pashler, H. (2008). Spacing effects in learning a temporal ridgeline of optimal retention. *Psychological Science*, 19(11), 1095–1102.

7.  Busch, B. & Watson, E. (2019), *The Science of Learning*, 1st ed. Routledge.

# CONTENTS

## Section 2.3   Making operational decisions ☑

## Section 2.4   Making financial decisions ☑

## Section 2.5   Making human resource decisions ☑

# MARK ALLOCATIONS

**Green mark allocations**[1] on answers to in-text questions throughout this guide help to indicate where marks are gained within the answers. A bracketed '1' e.g. [1] = one valid point worthy of a mark. In longer answer questions, a mark is given based on the whole response. In these answers, a tick mark[✓] indicates that a valid point has been made. There are often many more points to make than there are marks available so you have more opportunity to max out your answers than you may think.

# COMMAND VERBS

## Points-based questions

### Give

This question type will only appear in Section C of Paper 2. They require you to recall knowledge and will always be worth 1 mark.

### Identify

This question type requires you to find a piece of information from a chart, diagram, graph or other quantitative material. When answering these, you do not need to write in full sentences; just write down the correct piece of information. It will always be worth 1 mark and could appear in Sections B and C of either paper.

### Define

This requires you to give an accurate definition of a key term. It will only appear in Paper 2, in Section C. It will be worth 1 mark and will be used interchangeably with 'Give' questions.

### Calculate

Calculation questions will always be worth 2 marks. You do not get any marks for simply writing the formula. A correct answer will always score 2 marks, but ensure you show your working out. If your answer is incorrect you may get a mark for correct workings. If you provide multiple answers, the one on the answer line will be the one accepted by examiners. If the question asks for 2 decimal places, make sure you reflect this in your answer, or you will lose a mark.

### State

This 1 mark question tests the skill of application. It will be linked to a case study, so will appear in Section B or C of either paper. Your response **must** be in the context of the business in the case study or you will not gain marks.

### Explain

These questions are contextless so will only appear in Section A. They will ask you to explain an impact, benefit, drawback or method. You will need to make a valid point and then support it with two linked strands of development. To do this, you need to use clear connectives such as 'therefore', 'this leads to', 'because', 'so' and 'as a result'. Try to avoid the use of the word 'also' as this indicates you are moving onto a second point. Be careful of **Explain one method...** questions. Make sure you explain a method rather than a benefit or a drawback in this case. A benefit or drawback will not be answering the question.

### Outline

These questions will only appear in Sections B and C as they test your application skills. You will need to offer a method, impact, benefit or drawback as directed. This needs to be supported by one linked strand of development. Your answer must also be specific to the business in the case study. These will be worth 2 marks.

# Levels-based questions

## Discuss and Analyse

There will be one Discuss question in each paper, and it will be the last question in Section A, worth 6 marks. As it is in Section A, it is not linked to a case study, so will be generic in nature. There will be two Analyse questions, both of which will be in Section B. You can answer these questions by making one or two points. If you make one point, you need to develop that point with a minimum of five linked strands of development. If you make two points, you need the minimum of five linked strands across the two points made. By doing so, you will score highly in terms of analysis. There are no marks for evaluation in these questions, so if the question asks you to Discuss or Analyse a benefit, you should only talk about one or two advantages. Mentioning a drawback would be an invalid response (unless the question asks about an impact). The only difference between these question types is that Analyse questions test application instead of knowledge and therefore require you to make your response specific to the business in the case study.

## Justify

These questions involve making a choice between two options. You can score full marks by only discussing one of the options. When answering a justify question, you could adopt a three-paragraph approach, all of which should be applied to the business in the case study:

### Paragraph 1:
Select the option you think is best and state the benefit of that option. You should analyse the point you have made by developing it using connectives. Aim to have at least three linked strands of development.

### Paragraph 2:
Give a counter argument by recognising a drawback of the option you have chosen. Again, support your point with at least three linked strands of development.

### Paragraph 3:
This should be your conclusion and should be in the context of the business. Why is this option the best? What are the key points that have led you to that decision? One way you can show high level evaluative skills is to use the 'it depends on...' rule. What might your final decision depend on?

## Evaluation

Similar to a Justify question, you should adopt a three-paragraph approach. However, this time you will not have two options to select from. You must provide an argument in support of the statement in the question, again developed with at least three linked strands. The second paragraph should be a counter argument to the statement, in order to provide balance. This should be as developed as the first. In the conclusion, you should decide why one argument is stronger than the other. In doing so, what is the key point that has determined this and what might it depend on? It is important to ensure your response is applied throughout and that you use business terms to show your understanding.

# TOPICS FOR THEME 1
## INVESTIGATING SMALL BUSINESS 1BS0/01

## Information about Paper 1

**Written exam: 1 hour 30 minutes**
**90 marks**
**All questions are mandatory**
**50% of qualification grade**
**Calculators are permitted in this examination.**

### Specification coverage

Enterprise and entrepreneurship, spotting a business opportunity, putting a business idea into practice, making a business effective, understanding external influences on business.

The content for this assessment will be drawn from topics 1.1 to 1.5 in the specification.

### Assessment overview

The paper is divided into three sections:
Section A: 35 marks
Section B: 30 marks
Section C: 25 marks.

The paper will consist of calculations, multiple-choice, short-answer and extended-writing questions. Questions in Sections B and C will be based on business contexts given in the paper.

# THE DYNAMIC NATURE OF BUSINESS

**Businesses operate in dynamic markets, meaning that they have to cope with an ever-changing environment. These changes occur because customer wants are constantly evolving, often driven by changes in technology.**

To be successful, businesses must have an appreciation of these changes and develop or adapt products to meet these needs. This can lead to new business ideas and opportunities.

## Why new business ideas come about

### Original ideas

Some successful businesses emerge because the entrepreneur comes up with an original product that meets a need that is not serviced by any existing business.

### Obsolete products and services

A product becomes **obsolete** when it ceases to meet customers' needs. Needs can change for many reasons, but very often it can be due to advancements in technology. Keeping a product up to date with customer needs is important if a business wants to continue to be successful.

## Changes in technology

As technology develops, new opportunities arise that businesses can take advantage of. A forward-thinking business that embraces change, and is willing to try out new ideas, can gain a competitive advantage as more technologically advanced products will be sought after by the consumers. Technological advancements can also help a business to become more efficient in terms of production, allowing products to be manufactured more safely, more quickly and for less cost.

## Changes in what consumers want

The needs of customers are constantly changing. Businesses must adapt their products in line with demand to ensure they are meeting these needs and to prevent customers going to competitors. By doing so, new business opportunities arise through changes in fashion, the economy or in the lifestyle of society.

Explain **one** benefit to a business of understanding changes in what customers want. [3]

*Understanding change will allow a business to adapt their products so the needs of customers are met.[1] This will help to maintain, or increase, sales levels[1], which may lead to increased revenue for the business[1].*

# RISK AND REWARD

**When deciding whether to go ahead with a business venture, or when making business decisions, an entrepreneur considers the risks and rewards associated with it.**

Some businesses may be deemed riskier than others. Common examples of such business are those that face seasonal demand or operate in highly competitive markets.

## Risk

### Business failure
The ultimate risk that an entrepreneur faces when starting a business, is failure. A lot of businesses will fail because they will run out of funds and therefore cannot pay for everything they need to.

### Financial loss
Businesses risk losing any **capital investment** that the owner has put in personally if it were to fail. If the business has **unlimited liability**, the owner's personal assets would also be at risk if the business cannot pay all its debts.

### Lack of security
When an individual sets up a business, they do not have a guaranteed regular income. These also will not benefit from sick, holiday or maternity pay. This could make paying their own bills, such as a mortgage, very difficult with severe consequences for missing payments.

## Reward

### Profit
A business will make a profit when its revenue exceeds the total costs over a period of time. This would be the financial reward that most entrepreneurs will seek in return for the risks they take.

### Business success
Success comes in different ways for different entrepreneurs. For many it may be financial, however there are huge non-financial rewards such as having personal satisfaction in running a business that is performing well, doing good for society or gaining recognition through awards.

### Independence
Many entrepreneurs will value working for themselves and benefiting from the freedoms that this may bring, rather than working for someone else who may dictate their working hours. Independence also allows the entrepreneur to make all the key decisions which can be very rewarding.

Asra is thinking of setting up a fruit and veg stall at his local open-air market.

Outline **one** risk that Asra might face in setting up his market stall. [2]

*Asra may have to pay for his fruit and veg upfront even though he may not sell it all.[1] This means that he may make a financial loss.[1]*

# THE ROLE OF BUSINESS ENTERPRISE

## Purpose of a business

A business must provide what its customers want or need. A business will do this by producing **goods** or **services** themselves, or by buying them from a supplier in order to sell on to customers. These must be products that customers are willing to buy.

## Adding value

Added value is the difference between the **variable cost** of the product and the **price** that customers are willing to pay for it. It is achieved by either reducing the cost or by giving the customer a reason to accept a higher price. Added value can be achieved by the following methods:

### Convenience

A product that saves a customer time is one that may meet their needs better. Therefore, they will be willing to pay more for it.

### Branding

Building a strong brand name will give a business a good reputation and make its products more sought after. This allows the business to increase the price. Customers will pay a premium so they can have that branded product.

### Quality

A product that is of high quality, whether it be more durable or have superior function, will be able to be sold at a higher price. Customers will be willing to pay more for something that performs better.

### Design

A product that is more aesthetically pleasing will help it stand out from rival products.

### USP

A **unique selling point** is a characteristic or feature of a product that makes it different from all other products in the market. A USP can also be gained from having unique packaging or outstanding customer service compared to rivals. Customers are likely to pay more for something that is unique.

Explain **one** benefit to a business of adding value to its products. [3]

*By adding value, a business is able to charge more for its products[1], therefore they may see an increase in revenue[1], allowing a business to potentially increase its profits[1].*

# THE ROLE OF ENTREPRENEURSHIP

An entrepreneur is someone who starts and runs their own business. In doing so, it is important that the entrepreneur demonstrates the necessary skills to:

## Organise resources

An entrepreneur must manage many different resources. These include human resources and capital. Organising human resources involves the entrepreneur ensuring they get the best out of their employees. Organising capital involves managing the business' finances as well as all the resources used to research and develop the product or to provide the service.

## Make business decisions

Decisions are not always easy to make. As an example, an entrepreneur will need to decide what the aims of the business are, whether they need to employ people and what products to sell. If they are not decisive, they may miss opportunities. Showing initiative is a key skill as it allows the entrepreneur to stay ahead of competition.

Explain **one** reason why an entrepreneur will need to have strong leadership qualities. [3]

*An entrepreneur must be able to make risky decisions[1]. This is because a decision may involve the possibility of financial loss[1]. Without having the ability to take the initiative, an entrepreneur may not be able to make a decision and as a result will miss out on potentially profitable opportunities[1].*

## Take risks

Running a business venture is risky, but to be successful an entrepreneur must be able to acknowledge and evaluate these risks. Risks can be managed and steps can be taken to reduce them, but an entrepreneur cannot plan for every eventuality and must be prepared to accept the outcomes of their actions and decisions.

There are about three million active business in the UK. Of these, between 10% and 12% of business fail each year. There are about 350,000 new businesses registered in the UK each year. Half of these are likely to fail within three years.

# CASE STUDY

**Khadija runs a Dance and Performing Arts School, The Blue Ribbon Dance School, in her local village. Khadija has a passion for teaching and loves to see her pupils performing in local competitions and in local amateur dramatic shows. The dance school offers high quality training for all ages (toddlers through to adults) and abilities.**

Khadija decided to start up the Dance School back in 2015. She had been working in the local high school, teaching Dance as part of the school's GCSE PE programme. She very quickly realised that there was a lot of local talent, but more importantly she noticed just how many people enjoyed taking part.

After conducting some research, Khadija noticed that there were no other dance schools in the local area so decided to set up her own dance studio.

She wants to involve as many people from the local community as possible and as a result has deliberately kept her pricing low, making her lessons accessible to all. Since 2015, the school has been successful, with many pupils earning awards in competitions and former pupils having a career in the performing arts.

# EXAMINATION PRACTICE

1.  A games console manufacturer has updated its latest console with improved features.
    In what way has the manufacturer added value to its product?                    [1]
    A – By lowering the price of the console.
    B – By raising the price of the console.
    C – Through branding.
    D – With improved design.

2.  Which **two** of the following are examples of services.                        [2]
    A – Buying a new desk for your room from an online furniture store.
    B – Buying some sweets from the local convenience store.
    C – Paying a taxi driver for a lift to the airport.
    D – Paying a vet for an operation they performed on your pet.
    E – Visiting the local deli to purchase some cheese.

3.  Explain **one** method a business may use to add value to a product.             [3]

4.  Explain **one** reason why it is important that an entrepreneur can organise resources.   [3]

5.  Explain **one** advantage to an entrepreneur of running their own business.       [3]

**For the following questions you must refer to the case study on the previous page.**

6.  Outline **one** reason why Khadija came up with the idea for *The Blue Ribbon Dance School*.   [2]

7.  Analyse the risk that Khadija might face in running *The Blue Ribbon Dance School*.   [6]

8.  Evaluate whether profit is the main reward that Khadija seeks from running *The Blue Ribbon Dance School*.
    You should use the information provided as well as your knowledge of business.    [12]

## 1.2.1

# CUSTOMER NEEDS

Businesses must meet customer needs if they are to be successful. In providing products that customers find desirable, businesses will be meeting these needs.

### What do customers need?

Customers want a product that satisfies their need. When choosing which product to buy, there are a number of different factors that will influence their decision. These are: **price**, **quality**, **choice** and **convenience**.

### Price

Customers will demand value for money. Some customers will be prepared to pay a higher price if they feel the product is worth it. Other customers will purchase the product that has the lowest price. The business has to decide what their customers are willing to pay when setting the price.

### Choice

Customers will expect to be able to choose from a range of different products. The more choice they have, the more likely it is that their needs will be met.

### Quality

Customers will expect the product to be of a sufficient standard and the business must match these expectations. Whether the product is of a very high quality will be dependent on the expectations of the target market.

### Convenience

If businesses can make life easier for customers, then they are more likely to be able to meet their needs. For instance, the business could choose a location that is really accessible for customers.

---

Explain **one** benefit to a business of meeting customer needs. [3]

*By satisfying the needs of customers, a business will make customers happy.[1] Therefore they may see an increase in sales from repeat purchases and by attracting new customers.[1] As a result, this would help the business to survive and become successful[1].*

# MARKET RESEARCH

Satisfying customer needs is the key to success. One of the key reasons for carrying out **market research** is to find out information about what customers want. It will also give a business data on the market itself and any potential competitors.

## Purpose of market research

### To identify and understand customer needs

By carrying out market research, a business can ascertain exactly what the customer wants.

### To identify gaps in the market

By looking at what else is available in the market, a business can find out if there are other businesses who are selling similar products. If there are not, then the business may have a **gap in the market.**

### To reduce risk

Market research can help establish whether there will be sufficient demand for a product. Without finding out this information, a business may produce and sell a product that nobody wants!

### To inform business decisions

Gathering information on customers, market trends and competitors will allow a business to have a better understanding as to what products to sell, how it should promote them, where it should sell them and at what price.

Discuss the benefit to a business of identifying a gap in the market. [6]

*By identifying a gap in the market, a business will know that no other business is serving the needs of the customers[✓]. Therefore, by producing a product that does meet these needs they are unlikely to face much competition[✓]. This may lead to a large increase in sales and revenue for the business[✓], potentially increasing profit[✓].*

*Another benefit is that by being the only provider of a certain product, the business can charge a higher price[✓]. This is because if customers want the product, they will have to buy it from that business[✓]. This therefore leads to higher revenue made per sale[✓], potentially increasing overall profits[✓].*

*This type of question will be marked using a Levels Based Marks Scheme. See page 90 for details.*

'Discuss' questions can be answered in a number of ways. The key is to ensure that you have at least five linked strands of development across one or two valid points. To achieve this, you need to use clear connectives, such as 'therefore...', 'this leads to...', 'because...' etc.

# MARKET RESEARCH METHODS

When a business has decided what information will be helpful to them, they then need to decide how they will find out the information. They can gather information themselves or choose to use information that has already been collected by others.

## Primary market research

**Primary market research** is new information that is collected first-hand by the business. It includes carrying out a **survey**, asking people to fill out a **questionnaire**, holding **focus groups** and carrying out **observations**.

| **Benefits** | **Drawbacks** |
| --- | --- |
| • The information collected will be up to date. | • It can be time consuming to collect. |
| • The questions asked can be tailored to ask specific questions relevant to the business. | • The research is open to potential bias, depending on the sample used. |
| • It allows the business to have direct contact with existing and potential customers. | • Often more expensive. |

## What questions should a business ask?

When conducting primary market research, a business may want to find out information about their customers, their competitors and the market itself.
Questions they should find the answers to include:

**Customers:**
- What price would customers be prepared to pay for the product?
- What do customers like about the product?
- How can the product be improved to better meet customers' needs?
- What features of the product are most important to customers?
- What is the demographic of the likely target market?

**Competitors:**
- Who are the main rivals?
- What makes competitor products unique?
- Why might a potential customer choose to buy from a competitor?
- How are competitors' products priced?

**Market:**
- Are more people being attracted to the market or is demand dropping off?

## Secondary market research

**Secondary market research** is where a business gathers data that already exists as it has been collected by someone else. Examples include researching on the **Internet**, looking at **market reports** and accessing **government reports**.

**Benefits**
- It is usually cheaper than primary research.
- It can be less time consuming because information is more easily found.

**Drawbacks**
- The information gathered may not be specific or relevant to the business.
- The information may be out of date..

## Use of data

**Qualitative data** is based on people's feelings, judgements and opinions, and cannot be expressed in numerical form. **Quantitative data** is numerical and can therefore be more easily statistically analysed.

Market research will be more effective when a business uses a combination of both quantitative and qualitative data. Managers need to be able to explain the statistics and figures that have been collected. Qualitative data allows them to do this.

Market research is not effective if the data is unreliable.

Explain **one** impact of making decisions based on unreliable market research data.                    [3]

*If a business has unreliable data, then they may produce a product that isn't wanted[1]. This could be because they have not surveyed a representative sample of their target market[1]. This could mean a lot of money is wasted in producing these products[1], causing the business to have cash flow problems[1].*

## Social media and market research

The use of **social media** has had a positive impact when conducting research. Businesses have been able to collect first-hand information much more quickly (and more cheaply) than through traditional methods.

# MARKET SEGMENTATION

**Market segmentation** involves grouping customers together based on shared characteristics, wants and needs. Once the target segment is decided upon, the business must decide what their needs are and where to place their product in the market.

## How to segment the market

### Location

Grouping customers together based on where they live. The business may choose to focus on selling to people in certain areas.

### Income

Grouping customers based on how much money they earn. A business may be able to charge more to a higher income group.

### Lifestyle

Grouping customers based on their hobbies and interests or based on the way they live their lives (e.g. health conscious and active).

### Demographics

A business may decide to segment the market based on statistical data relating to the population. For instance, they may decide to target single parent families, or young couples.

### Age

Customers can be grouped by how old they are. Different age groups have common interests.

## Disadvantages of segmenting the market

**Narrowing the market**

By focusing on one market segment, a business will be restricting the overall number of customers that may be potentially attracted to the business. Also, they may miss out on opportunities that may arise within other segments had the business been focusing on the market as a whole. This can cause overall sales figures to fall.

**Cost**

Adapting promotions to suit each individual segment can cause costs to increase. This is because each campaign has to be slightly different to meet the exact needs of that segment.

**Need to re-evaluate**

Customers' characteristics and desires will change over time. Therefore, a business must continually review its activities in order to ensure that it is still attractive to all the different segments it is targeting.

Explain **one** benefit to a business of segmentation. [3]

*By segmenting the market, a business can meet the specific requirements of each segment[1]. It is able to do this by differentiating the product to meet their individual needs[1]. This will make the business' products more attractive to each segment[1], causing sales to increase[1].*

# MARKET MAP

A **market map** is a diagram that helps a business to position their product and others in a market. Products or brands are plotted against two variables, such as quality and price. The variables used will be based on the needs of the target market.

### Benefits of market mapping

Businesses are able to see if there is a part of the market where there are no products. This may mean that there is a **gap in the market** where customer needs are not being met. Market mapping also helps a business to find out who their closest rivals are and how they are perceived.

### Drawbacks of market mapping

Products are plotted on the diagram based on the opinions and perceptions of the person creating it. This may not reflect reality and businesses may make poor decisions as a result. A business that spots a gap in the market must be cautious. There may be a gap because there is no demand for the type of product that they have identified. Why are there few brands in the 'High price, low quality' quadrant?

### Example of a market map

The example below shows a market map for the car market. It compares a perceived quality of cars with the price charged to customers.

Outline **one** way in which Motor Ltd, a car manufacturer, could use this map. [3]

*Motor Ltd would be able to see that there is a section of the market that is not being catered for[1]. This area would be in the production of a high quality car, for a lower price[1]. If Motor Ltd can manufacture a vehicle that serves these customers, then it could be very successful[1].*

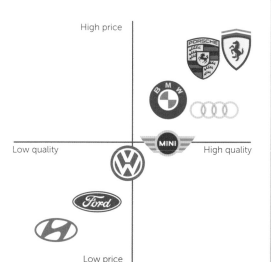

# THE COMPETITIVE ENVIRONMENT

A **competitive environment** is one in which there are many businesses selling similar products, each trying to attract the same customers. When operating in a competitive environment, a business should look at the following features to assess just how strong each competitor is:

## Quality

A business may choose to differentiate itself by producing products that are of a better quality. Therefore, customers will be attracted because they may seek a product that is superior in terms of function and durability.

## Customer service

Making a customer feel valued, by a business that is genuinely interested in their needs, can encourage repeat purchase. Word of mouth will help to build a positive reputation that will also attract new customers.

## Price

Some businesses will compete by being able to charge a low price for their product. This method relies on being able to produce the product cheaply so enough profit is made on each sale. It also means that a business must sell a larger quantity to make a large overall profit.

## Location

A customer may choose a business because it is more easily accessible than others in the market. This can include being located online.

## Product range

Having a wide product portfolio will give customers more choice. This may make them more likely to purchase from that business than from one that has a narrower product range.

Lyle has finished a mechanics apprenticeship. He is looking to set up his own car repair workshop but has identified that this is a very competitive market.

Outline **one** way in which operating in a competitive market will impact on his decision making.  [2]

*Lyle must differentiate his service from that of his rivals in order to be competitive.[1] He could do this by offering a free MOT test with every full service of a car[1]. Lyle will need to keep his costs of repairs low[1] so that he can be competitively priced when compared with other garages[1]. This means he may decide to use a cheaper supplier for parts and supplies.[1]*

# CASE STUDY

**Micah has a passion for the outdoors and recently finished studying at agricultural college, gaining qualifications in landscaping. Wanting to work for himself, he is thinking about setting up a garden and landscaping business in his home village of Chedgrave.**

Micah is looking to provide a complete range of hard and soft landscaping services, from the construction of walls, paths, fencing, roads, drives and tennis courts to ground clearance, turfing, tree planting, trimming and pruning. As a keen gardener himself, he is also looking to offer everyday gardening services, including mowing and lawn care. He has a detailed knowledge of plants and hopes to be able to offer horticultural services in time.

Before deciding whether to start, Micah has carried out some market research. To begin with, Micah looked on the Internet to see who his rival businesses would be. He found that there were several others already set up. To help him understand these competitors better, he plotted them on a market map based on his knowledge of these businesses. One of the competitors is Green Gardens Ltd, who offer all services at a competitive price. After creating the map, he concluded that there was a gap in the market for an upmarket service. As a result, he has decided that he must differentiate his service in some way in order to attract enough custom to make his business a success.

As part of his secondary research he also looked at population data from the most recent census. From that, he discovered that the village had a large proportion of elderly people. He believed that this proves that there would be a sufficient demand for his services.

He also surveyed his friends and family, as to their thoughts on him setting up this business. The results were very positive and encouraged him further that he could make this a successful business.

# EXAMINATION PRACTICE

1. Which **one** of the following would be a reason for creating a market map? [1]

    A – To find out what customer needs are.

    B – To identify any potential gaps in the market.

    C – To lower the breakeven level of sales.

    D – To show how much profit a business is making.

2. A business has decided to stock a wide product range as they believe that this is what customers want most.

    Which **one** of the following customer needs is the business trying to satisfy? [1]

    A – Choice

    B – Convenience

    C – Price

    D – Quality

3. Explain **one** benefit to a business of using a focus group. [3]

4. Explain **one** reason why a business might want to collect quantitative data. [3]

5. Explain **one** drawback to a business of using secondary market research. [3]

**For the following questions, refer to the case study on the previous page.**

6. State **one** way that Micah could meet the needs of his potential customers. [1]

7. Outline how Micah could segment the market. [2]

8. Analyse the impact on Micah's business from operating in a competitive market. [6]

9. Evaluate the effectiveness of the research that Micah conducted.

    You should use the information provided as well as your knowledge of business. [12]

# BUSINESS AIMS AND OBJECTIVES

An **aim** is what a business hopes to achieve in the long term. It can also be referred to as the goal of a business; it is the reason that the business is in existence. An **objective** is more specific and is the short-term target that a business seeks in order to fulfil their aim.

| Financial aims and objectives | Non-financial aims and objectives |
|---|---|
| These are aims and objectives that are related to money. They include the following: | These are aims and objectives that are not related to money. They include the following: |

### Financial aims and objectives

**Survival**
Businesses must bring in enough to cash to pay for all their bills so that they can continue to trade.

**Profit**
Business revenue that exceeds its costs creates profit. This is the main objective for many businesses, particularly those in the private sector.

**Sales**
Businesses set themselves a goal to increase the number of products or services they sell.

**Market share**
This is the percentage of the total sales in a market made by one business. Sometimes a business will prioritise increasing their market share so that they can become the dominant firm.

**Financial security**
Ensuring that a business generates enough revenue so that the business becomes self-sufficient. An entrepreneur may also want to have enough personal wealth so that they live comfortably without financial worry.

### Non-financial aims and objectives

**Social objectives**
A business may prioritise the people around them. They will try to do the right thing for society.

**Personal satisfaction**
It is the objective of some entrepreneurs to run a business in an area that interests them. They achieve satisfaction and happiness from owning their own business in that sector.

**Challenge**
Some entrepreneurs like the personal challenge that comes with setting up their own business and making a success of it.

**Independence and control**
Some entrepreneurs will like idea of being their own boss, so they set up and run their own business. By doing this, they have the freedom to make their own decisions and can control their own working hours.

Explain **one** reason why aims and objectives may differ between businesses. [3]

*A new start-up business may have to focus on survival whereas an established business may not[1]. This is because the new start-up won't have a loyal customer base yet so won't have the steady inflow of cash that an established business will have[1]. Therefore, it may be harder for a new start-up to break-even[1].*

# BUSINESS REVENUES, COSTS AND PROFITS

To be able to accurately calculate **profit**, a business will need to know its **revenue** and its **total costs**. If a business can calculate these then it can also carry out some analysis by looking at what profit it will make at different sales levels.

## Revenue

**Revenue** is also referred to as **sales revenue** or **turnover**. It is the total amount of income made from selling a product or service. It is calculated by using the following formula:

**Revenue = Selling price × Number of units sold**

## Fixed and variable costs

**Fixed costs** are those that do not change in line with changes in output. An example would be advertising costs.

**Variable costs** are those that will change directly with changes in output. An example would be raw materials. The formula for total variable costs is:

**Total variable costs = Variable cost per unit × Number of units sold**

## Total costs

**Total costs** are all the costs added together that a business incurs in making a product or providing a service.

**Total costs = Fixed costs + Variable costs**

1. Jasmeen runs a small handmade chocolate business. She has provided the following information:

   - Average selling price of a box of chocolates – £5.50
   - Fixed costs of running the business – £12,500
   - Variable cost for each box of chocolates – £2.00

   Calculate the total cost of producing 5,000 boxes of chocolates. [2]

   *Fixed costs = £12,500*

   *Variable costs = £2.00 × 5,000 = £10,000*

   *Total costs = Fixed costs + variable costs = £12,500 + £10,000 = £22,500*[2].

## Profit

**Profit** is made when the revenue received exceeds the total costs. If a business has total costs that are greater than revenue it is called a **loss**.

**Profit = Revenue – Total costs**

In the exam you will always be given full marks for giving the correct answer, regardless as to whether you have shown any workings out or not. However, it is a good idea to show workings out. If you make a mistake with the final answer you may still pick up a mark for showing your calculations.

2. Using the information on Jasmeen's business in Q1, calculate the profit made from producing and selling 5,000 boxes of chocolates. [2]

*Revenue = £5.50 × 5,000 = £27,500*

*Total costs = Fixed costs + variable costs = £12,500 + (£2.00 × 5,000) = £22,500*

*Profit = Revenue – total costs = £27,500 – £22,500 = **£5,000**[2].*

## Interest

When a business borrows money from the bank, the bank will charge them an **interest rate**. This is expressed as a percentage per annum. The formula used to calculate the interest rate charged on a loan is:

**(Total repayment – Borrowed amount) ÷ Borrowed amount × 100**

3. A business borrowed £15,000 and paid back a total of £15,900.

Calculate the rate of interest that the bank charged. [2]

*Interest rate = (£15,900 – £15,000) ÷ £15,000 × 100 = **6%**[2].*

In the exam you may be asked to demonstrate your quantitative skills. This could include calculating percentage increases. For example, if a business earned £5,000 profit in January, but earned £6,000 in February, what is the percentage increase?

*To calculate this, you need to use the following formula:*

(Difference in figures ÷ original figure) × 100

In this case it would be: (1,000 ÷ 5,000) × 100 = 20%

Profit has increased by 20%!

# BREAK EVEN

A firm will **break even** when it sells enough products to generate sufficient revenue to cover its total costs.

## Calculating breakeven

A new business must know how much it needs to sell so that it can ensure that the business is viable. A **break even analysis** is used to aid a business in making decisions about what price to charge, how much to produce and to help in managing costs.

The break even level of output is the number of products that a business needs to sell in order for revenue to equal total costs. It can be calculated using this formula:

**Break even = Fixed costs ÷ (Selling price − Variable cost per unit)**

1. Reanna runs a mobile dog grooming business. She has provided the following information:
   * Average amount paid per customer – £25
   * Fixed costs of running the business per year – £7,500
   * Variable cost of materials used for each dog grooming session – £10

Calculate the number of dog grooming sessions per year that Reanna will have to do in order to break even. [2]

*Break even = fixed costs ÷ (selling price – variable cost per unit)*

*£7,500 ÷ (£25 – £10)*

*= 500 dog grooming sessions per year[2].*

## Usefulness of break even

Break even analysis is particularly useful for new start-up businesses as it will allow them to see if their business is viable. This is because they will know how many products or services they need to sell to cover their costs. They can then decide whether that is an achievable amount.

Break even is used for 'what-if' analysis. A business can change the variables, such as the selling price and variable cost per unit, to see what impact that has on the level of break even. This will also tell the business what might happen to profit levels, so it can make important decisions related to price, production levels and costs.

## Break even charts

Break even can also be shown diagrammatically with the use of a **break even chart**. In this chart, a business will plot its costs and revenues at different output levels in order to find out the break even level of output.

When constructing a break even chart, revenue, total costs and fixed costs must each be plotted.

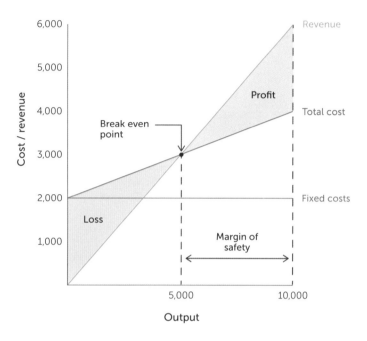

**Break even point:** This is also known as the **break even level of output**. As you can see, this particular business needs to sell 5,000 products in order to receive enough revenue to cover its total costs. At this point, profit would be £0; neither a profit nor a loss is made.

**Profit/loss:** Beyond the break even point, revenue exceeds total costs. Therefore, the business is making a profit at any output level above 5,000. Below the break even level of output, total costs are greater than revenue so the business is making a loss.

**Margin of safety: The margin of safety** is the difference between the actual output of a business and the break even level of output. If the business in the chart is producing 10,000 units then the margin of safety will be 5,000 units (10,000 − 5,000). This means that sales can drop by 5,000 units before a loss is made.

2. Explain **one** method a business could use to reduce its break even level of output. [3]

*Using cheaper raw materials in production of the product[1] will mean that variable costs per unit are lower[1]. This increases the difference between the selling price and the cost of making the product[1]. This will lower the amount needed to be sold to break even.*

*A business can reduce its break even by increasing the selling price[1]. Therefore, the difference between price and variable costs will be greater[1], meaning they need to sell fewer products or services to cover the fixed costs[1].*

# CASH AND CASH-FLOW

**Cash-flow** is the amount of money flowing into and out of a business over a period of time. Having enough cash is critical to a business. Many businesses fail because they do not have sufficient cash to pay all their bills.

## The importance of cash to a business

A business uses cash to pay for all its day to day expenses. This include paying its employees and paying for its supplies. Without workers, most businesses could not continue. Without supplies, the business could not produce its product or provide its service.

If a business does not have enough cash to pay for its bills when they are due, it is said to be **insolvent**. This will lead to the failure of the business.

## Difference between cash and profit

**Cash** is the amount of money that a business has available to pay for its day to day expenses. **Profit** is the difference between revenue and total costs. A profitable business can run out of cash. This is because a business records revenue as soon as a sale is made, but they may not receive actual payment immediately. In the interim period, large bills may become due.

1. Discuss the reasons why a business may encounter cash-flow difficulties. [6]

*One reason is because of seasonal demand[✓]. This means that a business may have periods in the year when demand is very low because of the nature of the product they are selling[✓]. This leads to the business not receiving many receipts during this time[✓]. They may then not have sufficient cash to pay for all the bills that they still need to pay[✓], causing cash-flow difficulties.*

*Another reason is that a business may have unfavourable credit terms with their suppliers and customers[✓]. This may mean that they pay their suppliers in cash when they order their supplies, whilst allowing customers a period of time before paying for the products they've bought[✓]. This means that the business will incur cash outflows whilst making the product and not receive any cash until long after[✓]. As a result, a business will have poor cash flow.*

*This type of question will be marked using a Levels Based Marks Scheme. See page 90 for details.*

In the answer given to the question above, you can see that two of the reasons given are seasonal demand and poor credit terms. As this was a 'Discuss' question, the response can be generic. If this was an 'Analyse' question it would be linked to a case study and you would have to apply your response to the business in the case study. Make sure you read it thoroughly as it will give you hints as to why the business had cash-flow difficulties. Other reasons could include:

• Unexpected changes in costs.
• Having too much cash tied up in stock that can't be sold.
• Unexpected changes in demand.
• Overtrading (spending too much on expansion).

## Cash-flow forecast

A **cash-flow forecast** is a prediction of future cash inflows and outflows for a business.

| £ | Jan | Feb | Mar | Apr |
|---|---|---|---|---|
| Total receipts | 110,000 | 90,000 | 70,000 | 80,000 |
| Total payments | 75,000 | 135,000 | 95,000 | 60,000 |
| Net cash-flow | 35,000 | (45,000) | (25,000) | 20,000 |
| Opening balance | 25,000 | 60,000 | 15,000 | (10,000) |
| Closing balance | 60,000 | 15,000 | (10,000) | 10,000 |

A business will use a forecast to spot, in advance, when it is likely to have cash-flow difficulties. Therefore, the business can take action to ensure that it does not run out of cash. In the example above, the business looks like it will have problems in March. Therefore, the business should take action to ensure that it doesn't encounter financial problems.

Remember the following!
An exam question could ask you to fill in the blanks on a cash-flow forecast:

- Net cash flow = total receipts − total payments.
- Closing balance = opening balance + net cash flow.
- Opening balance is always the same as the previous month's closing balance.

2. Calculate the missing figure from the cash-flow forecast below. [2]

| £ | Jun |
|---|---|
| Total receipts | ? |
| Total payments | 105,000 |
| Net cash-flow | 35,000 |
| Opening balance | 10,000 |
| Closing balance | 45,000 |

*Net cash flow = total receipts − total payments.*
*Total receipts = net cash-flow + total payments.*
*Total receipts = 35,000 + 105,000[1] = £140,000[2].*

## Improving cash-flow

**Better credit terms:** A business could encourage its customers to pay cash up front rather than offering them **trade credit**. It could also ask for a longer period of trade credit from its suppliers.

**Arranging finance:** A business could seek financial help from others in order to increase its receipts during periods of poor cash flow. This could be in the form of a bank **overdraft**.

**Better stock management systems:** A business could ensure that it does not have too much cash tied up in stock that doesn't sell by ordering only the amount of materials that it needs, rather than holding stock just in case.

# SOURCES OF BUSINESS FINANCE

All businesses need finance whether they are just starting-up or whether they are well established. Businesses need finance to expand the business, invest in new products and technologies as well as for paying for everyday expenses.

## Short-term sources of finance

**Short-term sources of finance** are generally used when a business needs to raise small amounts of finance or when they can be repaid back very quickly. They are used for things like purchasing stock or resolving a short-term cash flow problem. Sources include:

**Overdraft:** An **overdraft** is an agreement with the bank that allows a business to spend more than they have in their bank account up to an agreed limit. This must be repaid to the bank.

**Trade credit: Trade credit** is offered when a business receives goods from a supplier but doesn't actually have to pay for them until after an agreed amount of time (e.g. 28 days).

---

Explain **one** benefit to a business of using an overdraft. [3]

*The business will only pay interest on the amount of the overdraft that they use[1]. This means that if only a small amount is used, then the total repayment will be lower than using other forms of finance[1]. This can help to keep costs low[1].*

## Long-term sources of finance

**Long-term sources of finance** are generally used when a business requires a large amount of finance over a long period of time, for example when a business is expanding. Sources include:

**Personal savings:** The owners of sole traders and partnerships may choose to invest their own funds into the business. A benefit of this is that it does not need to be repaid, but it does mean that the owner won't have the funds available for anything else.

**Venture capital: Venture capital** is finance raised from successful entrepreneurs, banks and private equity companies in return for a share of the business, which means the owner loses some control. However, a business may benefit from the experience of the venture capitalists.

**Share capital: Share capital** is finance raised from selling shares in the business. This means that some control is lost. Only limited companies can raise finance in this way. This method allows large amounts to be raised.

**Loans:** A business will borrow money from a bank. They will make monthly repayments back to the bank, which will include **interest**.

**Retained profit:** Profit made that is then reinvested back into the business. Using **retained profit** could reduce costs and reduce cash inflows since no interest has to be paid to banks, but they will no longer have these funds for other needs.

**Crowd funding: Crowd funding** involves a business making an online appeal to investors who each invest small amounts of money, in order to raise a large amount overall. If the target amount of finance is not reached, the business does not get the money and their reputation may be harmed.

# CASE STUDY

***Gibbs Bakery Ltd* is a family run bakery that has been producing high quality breads and confectionery produce since 1872.**

The business prides itself on the quality of their produce. Their breads and cakes are baked daily using traditional recipes that have been handed down from generation to generation. Products are made without the use of additives or artificial preservatives, by a dedicated team of bakers who have a wealth of experience in the industry. Robert Gibbs, the current owner, is proud of their reputation for producing top quality goods and is pleased that they are one of the market leaders in the area for artisan bakery.

The following financial information relates to Robert's business:

- Variable cost of making each item: £0.40
- Average selling price of the bakery products sold: £1.65
- Fixed costs per day: £1,250
- Number of products sold per day: 1,300
- Daily break even level of output: 1,000

The bakery has a shop in the village of Mere, situated on the Wiltshire border. As well as this, the bakery delivers their breads and confections all over Wilshire, Dorset and Somerset. Their vans take fresh produce to shops and local businesses across the region on a daily basis in order to keep shelves stocked with the highest quality goods.

More and more retail outlets are requesting daily deliveries from *Gibbs*. In order to meet this demand, Robert has decided to purchase a new fleet of vans. To fund this venture, he is looking to raise a substantial amount of finance. At times, Robert experiences high demand for his goods, often selling out before the end of the day.

# EXAMINATION PRACTICE

1. Which **one** of the following would be classed as a variable cost for a business? [1]

   A – Advertising      B – Insurance      C – Raw materials      D – Salaries

2. Which **two** of the following are classed as non-financial objectives of a business? [2]

   A – Challenge      B – Personal satisfaction      C – Profit      D – Sales      E – Survival

3. Explain **one** reason why survival is a particularly important objective for new start-up businesses. [3]

4. Explain **one** reason why cash is important to a business. [3]

5. The graph below shows a monthly break even diagram for a business. Using this information, calculate the break even level if fixed costs were to increase to £2,250 per month. [2]

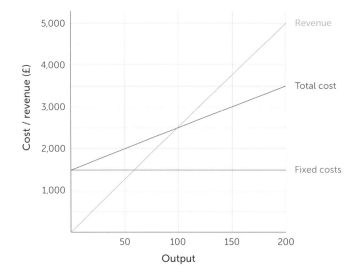

**For the following questions you must refer to the case study on the previous page.**

6. State **one** financial objective that Robert might have for *Gibbs Bakery*. [1]

7. Calculate the profit that *Gibbs Bakery* makes each day. [2]

8. Calculate the margin of safety for *Gibbs Bakery*. [2]

9. To finance the investment, Robert is considering two options:
   - Option 1: Using retained profit.
   - Option 2: Using a bank loan.

   Justify which of the two options *Gibbs Bakery* should choose. [9]

10. Evaluate the most effective method that *Gibbs Bakery* could use to increase profits.
    You should use the information provided as well as your knowledge of business. [12]

# LIABILITY AND OWNERSHIP

When an entrepreneur decides to start up a business, they have a number of different options for its formation. Each option will have an impact on the legal status of the business.

## Liability

If a business owner (entrepreneur) has **unlimited liability**, then they and the business are seen as the same legal entity. This is known as an **unincorporated** business. Any debts that the business has, will be the total responsibility of the owner. If the business cannot pay the debts off, then the owner may have to sell personal possessions to clear them. If an entrepreneur has **limited liability**, then they are seen as separate from the business in the eyes of the law. This is called **incorporation**, where the debts of the business are not regarded as personal debts of the owner. The entrepreneur is only liable for the amount of money that they have personally invested.

## Types of ownership

### Sole trader

An unincorporated business which has only one owner.

**Advantages**
- Quick and easy to set up.
- Sole trader keeps all the profits.
- Sole trader makes all the decisions.
- Business' financial information is kept private.

**Disadvantages**
- Sole trader faces unlimited liability.
- May be more difficult to raise finance.
- Business may not run if sole trader is off sick or takes holiday.

## Partnership

An unincorporated business which has two or more owners who share the risk.

**Advantages**
- Each partner could contribute finance.
- Each partner can bring ideas and different skills.
- The workload can be shared amongst different partners.
- Business' financial information is kept private.

**Disadvantages**
- Partners face unlimited liability.
- There may be disagreements between the partners.
- Profits are shared amongst partners according to agreed ratios.

## Private limited company (ltd)

An incorporated business which is owned by shareholders. Shares can only be sold privately, usually to friends and family.

**Advantages**
- Easier to raise finance by selling shares.
- Owners have limited liability.

**Disadvantages**
- Overall control could be lost.
- The company's accounts and financial information is not private.
- More legal paperwork involved when setting up as it is more complex.

# FRANCHISING

An entrepreneur has the option to set up as an independent business or set up as a **franchise**. A **franchisee** is licensed to sell the products or services of an already established business, known as the **franchisor**.

## Franchise

The license given by the franchisor allows the new owner to trade using the name, products and equipment of the franchisor, whilst remaining independent. However, the franchisor will charge a fee in return, as well as taking a share of the business' revenues, known as a **royalty**.

## Why start as a franchise?

By setting up as a franchise rather than an independent business, the new owner is hoping to reduce the risks faced when starting a business. Risk is reduced because of the following reasons:

- **Brand name is already established:** This will mean that customers will recognise the business name and its products, so may be more likely to purchase products. The business will already have an established customer base.

- **Access to established products and processes:** Not only will the franchisee be able to sell products that customers already know about, they will also gain access to the franchisor's processes and equipment.

- **Franchisor provides training:** The franchisor will provide ongoing support for the franchisee. This is because it is in their interest that the business is successful too.

- **Franchisor undertakes advertising and promotion:** This means that there is one less thing for franchisee to do. The franchisor can afford to undertake expensive advertising that the individual owner may not be able to pay for if they were completely independent.

Discuss the drawback to an owner of setting up a business as a franchisee. [6]

*One drawback is that a franchisee cannot choose where to get supplies from[✓]. This means that they have no room to shop around to find a cheaper supplier[✓], meaning that they are unable to reduce their variable cost by finding someone selling supplies for less[✓]. Therefore, they may be unable to change the price that the product is sold for[✓], which could make them uncompetitive against other local independent competitors[✓]. This could have a negative impact on sales levels[✓], causing the business not to sell enough products to break even[✓].*

*Other drawbacks include expensive initial start-up fees, royalty fees to the franchisor regardless of profits made and other restrictions placed on the franchisee such as choice of location.*

# BUSINESS LOCATION

The location that a business chooses can have a huge impact on the success of a new start-up. There are various factors that will determine which location is best. These vary in importance depending on the nature of the business.

## Factors influencing business location

### Proximity to market

For some businesses, being close to where the customers are will be the most important factor. By doing this, it can raise awareness of the business and help it to become established. This is particularly important for retail businesses.

### Proximity to materials

Some businesses may require large bulky raw materials, such as timber, to be able to produce their product. Transporting the supplies to the business may be expensive, so to keep costs down businesses may choose to locate close to where they can easily access the materials they need.

### Proximity to competitors

Some businesses will choose to locate far away from their competitors so that they are the only supplier of a good or service in that area. Others may choose to locate close to their rivals as this is where customers are likely to be. For example, a shopping mall.

### Proximity to labour

It can be important that there are sufficient available workers close by who have the skills that a business needs. A business needs to locate where people are willing and able to work.

## Nature of the business activity

The most important of the four factors above depends on the nature of the activity that the business is involved in. A manufacturing firm may need to be close to supplies, while a service sector business will need to be close to customers. The proximity of competitors may be even more important.

---

Explain **one** impact of the Internet on the location decision of a business. [3]

*Developments in Internet speeds and availability, and the rise of e-commerce has meant that entrepreneurs can set-up their businesses from home[1]. This is because they can sell products via their website or that of other third parties rather than having a physical retail outlet[1]. This has meant that businesses only need somewhere to store their goods which doesn't need to be an expensive high street location[1]. This would reduce their fixed costs[1], therefore increasing profitability[1].*

# THE MARKETING MIX

The **marketing mix** is a combination of four factors – 'the four Ps' (**product**, **price**, **place** and **promotion**) which a business uses in order to persuade customers to buy their product. The mix will change over time and each element has an influence on the others.

## Price

A business must set a price that enables it to make a profit. Therefore, it is important that an entrepreneur is aware of all the costs involved. A new start-up will often sell their products at a low price in order to attract people to purchase their products. A product that is of a superior quality may be priced highly compared to competitor products.

## Place

A business must think about distribution. Distribution concerns how a product eventually gets to the customer from a producer. Within this element, businesses have to decide whether to sell directly to the customer, either by having a physical location or via the Internet, or they could choose to use wholesalers and retailers.

## Promotion

A business needs to promote itself to raise customer awareness of the products that are available. This helps to increase sales and build a brand image. There are many forms of promotion which include advertising, special offers and public relations.

## Product

After conducting market research, a business will know the needs of their customers. The product, through its features, design and function should meet those needs. The business needs to consider what will make its product different from others on the market.

For more details on the four Ps, see Section 2.2.

## Influences on the marketing mix

**The competitive environment:** If a competitor is selling a similar product at a lower price, then a business may have to decrease the price they charge. They may also have to develop new products if rivals introduce their own, newer and better products onto the market.

**Technology:** New technology has enabled businesses to develop more innovative products, particularly in technology markets. It has also allowed businesses to undertake promotion via digital communications, such as social media sites. Developments in the use of the Internet has allowed e-commerce to grow. Businesses are now choosing to sell products online rather than having a physical store.

Explain **one** impact of changing customer needs on the marketing mix of a business. [3]

*As customer trends change, a business may need to update the features of its product[1]. Therefore, there is a cost implication in designing and updating the product[1], meaning that the business may have to increase the price[1]. Increasingly, customers are utilising social media sites[1]. As a result, businesses need to ensure that they are promoting themselves via this medium[1]. This will allow a business to stay current and help to maintain its brand image[1].*

# BUSINESS PLANS

A **business plan** is a working document that details the objectives that a business wants to achieve and how it will set about achieving them. It looks at all aspects of the business so that risk is reduced, giving the business a greater chance to succeed.

## The role and importance of a business plan

A business plan will detail what the idea of the business is. It gives the entrepreneur a guide to follow and gives other stakeholders a clear vision. It will involve all aspects of the business, therefore forcing the entrepreneur to think carefully about the opportunity. For example, it will help to identify:

- The business idea
- The business' aims and objectives
- The target market of the business
- The business' marketing plan
- Forecasted revenues, costs and profit
- Cash-flow predictions
- How the business is to be financed
- Where the business plans to locate
- How the product is to be produced or the service provided
- The marketing mix

Explain **one** reason why a bank might be interested in a business plan. [3]

*A business may be asking the bank to lend them some money to cover the start-up costs[1]. Before the bank lends any money, they will want to know that the business has a good chance of success[1]. As the business plan details financial forecasts, the bank can see whether they believe the business will have enough money to cover the repayments[1].*

## The purpose of planning business activity

### Minimising risk

Producing a business plan cannot guarantee that a business will be successful. There will always be the risk that something unforeseen could happen which could negatively impact on the business. However, by producing a business plan, an entrepreneur will be thinking about a lot of different scenarios and how the business could deal with them. Therefore, they will be prepared for a lot of eventualities.

### Obtaining finance

Any potential investor will want to know that their investment is as secure as possible. Although risk cannot be eliminated, by producing a business plan, an entrepreneur can show potential investors that every aspect of the business has been thought about and that costly mistakes will be avoided

# CASE STUDY

Graham Munroe started *Woodkit Ltd* a few years ago. It is a family run business with strong values. They are a major internet retailer and wholesaler of many international brands of wooden planes, tanks, boats and accessories. The business has the UK's widest product range selling over 4,000 exquisite, precision-made items to markets at home and abroad. They sell both vintage and contemporary models, catering for all needs, tastes and budgets.

At *Woodkit*, Graham places a considerable amount of value on making customers happy. They have a large number of repeat customers, particularly those who are enthusiastic collectors. Graham encourages customers to get in touch regarding any queries that they may have. They also keep customers regularly informed about what the business is up to through a regular e-newsletter. Signing up for the e-newsletter gives customers access to all the business' special offers and member benefits. They have also set up a Facebook page so that customers can be part of *Woodkit's* online community.

*Woodkit* have a dedicated website which allows the customers to see all the products that are on offer as well as all the international brands that they also sell. Customers can order directly from the website.

Graham recognised that there was a big market for model-making and accessories in both the USA and Australia. They sell extensively to customers in these countries, giving free delivery for orders over a certain weight.

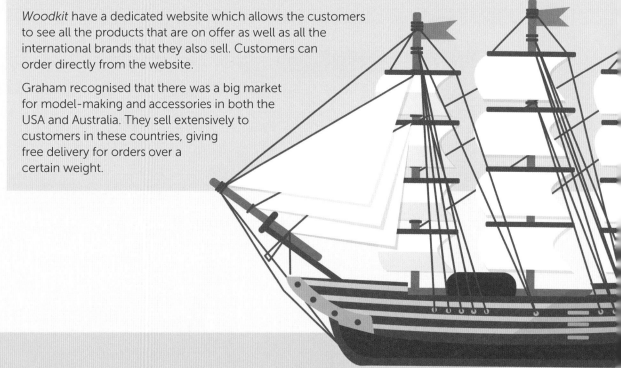

# EXAMINATION PRACTICE

1.  Which **one** of the following is part of a business' marketing mix? [1]
    A – Partnership
    B – People
    C – Place
    D – Profit

2.  Which **two** of the following would be the most important factors influencing the location of a business that manufactures buses for a national bus chain? [2]
    A – Proximity to city centre bus stations
    B – Proximity to competitors
    C – Proximity to labour
    D – Proximity to materials
    E – Proximity to users of public transport

3.  Explain **one** benefit to a business of setting up as a franchise rather than independently. [3]

4.  Explain **one** reason why locating away from competitors may be important for a business. [3]

**For the following questions you must refer to the case study on the previous page.**

5.  Outline **one** reason that *Woodkit's* range of stock could give it an advantage over competitor businesses. [2]

6.  Outline how technology has impacted the marketing mix of *Woodkit*. [2]

7.  Analyse the impact on *Woodkit* of being a private limited company. [6]

8.  Analyse the benefit to Graham of creating a business plan before the start-up of *Woodkit Ltd*. [6]

9.  Evaluate the importance of product in *Woodkit's* marketing mix.
    You should use the information provided as well as your knowledge of business. [12]

# BUSINESS STAKEHOLDERS

A **stakeholder** is an individual or group that has an interest in a business. Each stakeholder will have a different objective and is affected in different ways by the decisions a business makes. The interests that each stakeholder has, often come into conflict with each other.

## Different objectives of stakeholders

| Stakeholder | What they want from the business |
|---|---|
| Shareholder (Owner) | This group will commonly want the business to be financially successful so they can maximise the profits that are made. |
| Employees | Workers will want job security and financial reward in return for their labour. |
| Customers | Customers will want the product or service to fulfil their needs. They will expect good customer service and value for money. |
| Managers | Those in charge will want the business to be successful as it reflects well on them. They will also want financial reward for their work. |
| Suppliers | Suppliers will want the business to be successful, so they continue to receive orders. They will also want to be paid on time. |
| Local community | Local residents will want the business to be successful, so it continues to offer employment. They will also want the business to do good for their community. |
| Pressure groups | These organisations will want businesses to behave in an ethically and environmentally friendly manner. These can include trade unions who may campaign for workers' rights. |
| The government | The government will want businesses to be successful so that they continue to employ people. Businesses also pay tax to the government. |

Explain **one** reason why a business may experience stakeholder conflict. [3]

*The owners of a business will want to keep costs to a minimum while employees will want as high a wage as possible[1]. This means they will be in conflict because both objectives cannot be met[1]. As a result, either the employees will become dissatisfied, impacting on the customer service offered to customers, or the owners have to sacrifice some profit to keep workers motivated[1].*

*The shareholders may be in conflict with the owners over what happens to the profit that the business makes[1]. This is because the shareholders will want to receive as much of the profits in the form of dividends as possible[1]. However, the managers will want to retain the profits to finance growth[1].*

## Stakeholders and businesses

The owners and managers of a business will have a controlling influence on its activity, but they cannot ignore the other stakeholders as they have an influence on how the business operates:

- A business cannot ignore its customers. If they are not listened to, they will purchase products from rivals instead.
- A business needs a happy and motivated workforce so must consider their needs.
- Not paying attention to the needs of suppliers can lead to poor relationships with them.
- Ignoring the wishes of the local community and pressure groups could cause the business to develop a negative reputation.

# TECHNOLOGY AND BUSINESS

As technology advances, it presents businesses with many opportunities in terms of innovating products and production processes. However, those businesses that do not embrace technology and are slow to develop with it, can very quickly become uncompetitive.

## Different types of technology used by business

### E-commerce

**E-commerce** is the buying and selling of goods and services over the internet. It also allows customers to make purchases at any time of day and at their own convenience.

### Digital communication

**Digital communication** involves making contact with customers electronically. This can be done through email, e-newsletters, websites, mobile apps, live-chat and video calls.

### Social media

**Social media** has provided businesses with a cheap and efficient way of communicating with customers, or to gather feedback via polls. Information can be regularly and quickly updated. It also allows users to communicate with other users about a product.

### Payment systems

Customers now have the ability to use **electronic payment systems** to transfer money very quickly and safely, allowing much more convenient purchasing of products. Examples include contactless card or smartphone payments, chip and pin and online payments.

## How technology influences business activity

**Sales:** Embracing advancements in technology can help increase sales. This could be because the business is using e-commerce to sell to a much wider potential market. It can also occur because the business has used technology to be innovative with its products in a way that appeals to customers.

**Costs:** Technology has enabled businesses to be more efficient and make cost savings because:
- Firms that sell purely on the Internet do not need to pay for expensive shop locations.
- The use of technology in automating the production process means less money is required for employee wages.
- The use of social media and digital communications means more expensive, traditional forms of promotion are not required. This may have included postal and billboard marketing.

## Impact on the 4Ps

**Product:** Products have become more innovative and customers have more choice.

**Price:** Cost savings have allowed prices to be lowered.

**Promotion:** Using digital channels to promote rather than traditional methods.

**Place:** A large number of businesses are choosing to locate online.

---

Explain **one** drawback that advancements in technology might have on a business. [3]

*A business may need to invest heavily in technology in the first place which can be very expensive[1]. This is because staff may also need training[1] which can increase costs[1] well beyond that of the initial investment in new technology, equipment or machinery.*

# LEGISLATION AND BUSINESS

There are various pieces of **legislation** that govern how businesses behave. Consumer law ensures that buyers are protected from being exploited by businesses. Employment law governs how businesses interact and deal with their workers.

## The purpose of legislation

### Principles of consumer law

Consumer law is enforced to ensure that consumers are protected from malpractice by businesses. It protects consumers by addressing the quality of products and the rights of the consumer by stating that:

- Products should be fit for purpose.
- Products must be of satisfactory quality.
- Products must be as described.

Consumers have the legal right to their money back, or to have their product repaired or replaced if the business does not meet these principles.

### Principles of employment law

Employment legislation is enforced in order to protect workers. Various laws are in place to stop employees from being exploited by their employers. It covers the following areas:

- **Recruitment:** Businesses must ensure that employees have a legal right to work in the UK. This involves completing checks on new employees.
- **Discrimination:** A business must not be discriminatory against employees. This includes discriminating because of age, gender, race, religion, sexual orientation or because of disability. The business must ensure that they pay people the same amount of money for the same work completed.
- **Pay:** All employees are entitled to receive a minimum wage. Workers aged over 25 years old and above are entitled to receive the National Living Wage, which is slightly more than the National Minimum Wage.
- **Health and safety:** All workers have the right to be kept safe whilst at work. Businesses must carry out risk assessments of workspaces to ensure that risks are controlled and minimised.

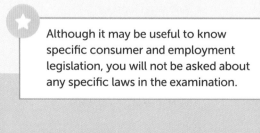

Although it may be useful to know specific consumer and employment legislation, you will not be asked about any specific laws in the examination.

## The impact of legislation on business

Complying with consumer and employment legislation gives a business some advantages:

- By complying with consumer legislation, a business will gain a positive reputation which will help future sales.
- By doing the right thing by customers, a business will have better relationships with this stakeholder group, potentially leading to higher customer loyalty.
- As employees will feel happier and better protected, they may be more motivated and therefore more productive.
- A business will be seen as a good employer and as such, will likely find it easier to recruit the people they need as well as retaining the staff they already have.

Discuss the drawbacks that legislation can have on a business. [6]

*In complying with legislation, a business may incur additional expenditure[M]. This is because they will have to keep up to date with changes in legislation which may also involve training staff[M]. This would increase the total costs to the business[M]. As a result, they would have to sell more products in order to break even[M]. This could make it harder for a business to survive in their market[M].*

*Another drawback is that if they failed to comply, the business could see damage to its reputation[M]. For example, if there was an accident to an employee at work and it was discovered that the business hadn't complied with health and safety legislation, they may have to pay compensation to the injured party[M]. As a result, the business could get negative publicity[M]. This may not only have an impact on future recruitment, but also on sales levels[M] as customers decide to purchase from a more reputable business[M]. This could have consequences to a business in terms of its survival[M].*

This question asks for a drawback. If this is the case for a 'Discuss' question, you must only write about the negatives. This question type does not require a balanced argument. To best answer this question, you must discuss either one or two drawbacks.

In this question you could have used the following drawbacks as alternative responses:

- Additional cost of administration.
- Additional cost of PPE equipment to keep staff safe.
- Additional expenditure due to National Living Wage.

# THE ECONOMY AND BUSINESS

Businesses need to consider changes that are happening in the wider economy. These changes can have a lasting impact on the performance of a business.

## Changing levels of consumer income

**Consumer income** (also known as **disposable income**) is the amount of money that consumers have left to spend after they have paid for all their living expenses and bills. Economic variables affect the level of disposable income through:

- Changes in the level of taxation.
- Changes in the level of unemployment.
- Changes in the interest rate.
- Changes in exchange rates.

Income levels in an economy will have a significant impact on the level of **demand**. If consumers have more disposable income, then the level of demand will increase. This will lead to a business' sales level increasing.

## Unemployment

**Unemployment** exists in an economy when there are people of working age who want to work but cannot find a job. High levels of unemployment can be negative for a business because:

- Lots of consumers will have less disposable income.
- The level of demand in an economy will fall.
- Sales levels will decrease.
- As demand and sales fall, businesses may need fewer workers, so unemployment rises further.

In times of low unemployment, consumer incomes are high meaning they spend more money on goods and services. This will increase demand in an economy. However, businesses will find it harder to recruit people with the right skills.

## Government taxation

The government taxes individuals on the income they earn. If they increase the level of income tax, then consumers will have less disposable income. Businesses must pay corporation tax, which is based on profits. This increases the costs to a business. VAT is charged on most goods and services. If this increases, it makes the products more expensive.

Explain **one** benefit of high unemployment in an economy to a business. [3]

*One benefit is that recruitment may be easier for a business[1]. This is because there are a large number of people looking for a job[1]. Therefore, when a business is looking to recruit, there may be a large pool of potential candidates to select from, often with better qualifications than in times of low unemployment[1], increasing the chance that the business gets the best person for the job[1].*

## Inflation

**Inflation** is the general rise in the price level of goods and services within an economy. It represents the **cost of living**. When inflation increases, it means that the average prices of goods and services have been increasing at a faster rate compared to average earnings. This will have an impact on the costs of the business and the **purchasing power** any of **disposable income** consumers have.

### Costs to the business

As the price level in an economy will be increasing, suppliers are likely to put their prices up. This increases the cost to the business. As a result, this could have a negative impact on a business' profit levels unless they increase their own prices too.

### Consumer income

As prices of goods and services increase, consumers will have less disposable income. This means that demand will start to fall. If businesses choose to increase prices because their costs are increasing, it begins to perpetually worsen the situation.

## Changes in interest rates

**Interest rates** affect the cost of borrowing. This includes loans, mortgages and savings.

### Increase in interest rates

An increase in interest rates will increase the cost of borrowing to both businesses and consumers and will have the following impacts:

- Businesses who have taken out loans may see an increase in costs.
- Businesses are less likely to borrow money as it is now more expensive to do so.
- Consumers will have less disposable income as they have to repay more on any borrowed money and may be more inclined to save money with more favourable rates.

### Decrease in interest rates

The cost of borrowing is reduced and will have the following impacts:

- Business costs will decrease for those that have borrowed money.
- More businesses will be encouraged to borrow and spend money as it may be cheaper to do so.
- Consumers will be more inclined to spend money as borrowing money from banks or spending on credit cards will be cheaper.

## Exchange rates

An **exchange rate** is the value of one currency in terms of another.

### Impact of an increase in the value of the £

- Cheaper to import materials from abroad.
- Poor for exporters as the price of exports will rise.
- Domestic businesses suffer as customers buy cheaper products from abroad.

### Impact of a decrease in the value of the £

- Costs more to import materials from abroad.
- Good for exporters as the price of exports in terms of foreign currencies falls.
- Good news for domestic businesses as foreign imports become more expensive.

If £1 = $1.5, calculate:

1. How much will a product priced at £35 be in dollars ($)? [2]
2. How many $45 products can be purchased with £450? [2]

1. £35 × 1.5[1] = $52.50[2]
2. 450 × 1.5 = 675 ÷ 45[1] = 15[2]

# EXTERNAL INFLUENCES

External influences are those factors outside of a business' control that will either present an opportunity that the business can take advantage of, or will pose a threat to a business' survival. These external influences include changes in technology, legislation and the economy.

## Business responses to changes in technology

### New technology is developed

- Businesses should invest in research and development so that they can create new products and remain competitive.
- Investment in new machinery helps to reduce production costs. This allows a business to become more competitive.
- Improvements in communications and videoconferencing technology can increase the amount of homeworking. Less expensive office space is required by the business, reducing overall costs.
- Production of products that have become obsolete may have to stop.

## Business responses to changes in legislation

Discuss how a business may react to changes in consumer legislation that make it more difficult to sell a product. [6]

*One response is to stop selling the product[M]. As a result, they may have to spend money on researching and developing appropriate modifications, or a brand new product[M]. This may involve a business having to raise some finance to be able to fund the research[M]. Consequently, the business may find itself in debt[M].*

*Another response could be to enter new markets where there is less legislation on selling the product[M]. This may involve retraining staff and moving production locations[M], which would be costly[M], but would allow the business to continue to sell their product[M].*

*Tick marks are indicative only. Refer to the band descriptions and levels of response guidance for extended response questions on page 90.*

## Responses to change in the economic climate

### A rise in economic activity

Demand will be increasing so this could be the right time to invest and grow the business. Therefore, a business may:

- Recruit extra staff
- Invest in new equipment
- Research and develop more products
- Spread risk by entering different markets

### A fall in economic activity

Demand in the economy will be lower. Businesses may react by:

- Concentrating on their core activities
- Cutting investment and spending
- Reducing the size of the workforce
- Lowering prices to remain competitive

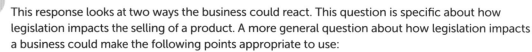

This response looks at two ways the business could react. This question is specific about how legislation impacts the selling of a product. A more general question about how legislation impacts a business could make the following points appropriate to use:

- Change company policy to adhere to changes in employment and consumer law.
- Investing in health and safety measures to ensure employees and customers are kept safe.

# CASE STUDY

**The *Waveney House Hotel* is a family run hotel situated in the picturesque Waveney Valley. It boasts a superb river location with stunning views across the surrounding countryside.**

The hotel offers 12 luxury bedrooms, all with en-suite bathrooms. Each are individually styled. Two of the suites not only contain a four-poster-bed but also have exceptional views across the river and Gillingham marshes. The hotel contains the top-class *Staithe Restaurant* and *Riverside Bar* offering a range of seasonal dishes using locally sourced meat, fish and vegetables. Meals are prepared and cooked to order, and are tailored to meet any dietary requirements. The hotel attracts many tourists, from both the UK and mainland Europe, particularly those on boating holidays as there are local moorings available.

As well as targeting tourists, the hotel also targets the events and functions markets as it boasts its own large function room complete with bar, lounge area, stage and dance floor. It forms an ideal venue for conferences, meetings, weddings, birthday parties and other special occasions.

The hotel has embraced technology in how it communicates with customers. It has a fully informative website detailing everything about their accommodation, dining and function services. The website also allows customers to book directly online and via other travel sites such as booking.com. It also has a link to Tripadvisor, a review website, so that customers can see what other guests thought of their time at the hotel. There is an e-brochure that customers can download which provides them with more detailed information on all the hotel's services. The Waveney House Hotel also utilises Facebook and Twitter to inform customers about the latest events and offers. The hotel has to also pay strict attention to legislation, particularly around the serving of food and drink. In recent months they have also had to respond to new legislation in terms of keeping its staff and customers safe.

# EXAMINATION PRACTICE

1.  Which **one** of the following is true when the pound (£) falls in value compared to the US dollar ($)?  [1]

    A – It benefits a UK manufacturer who imports raw materials from abroad.

    B – It is bad for UK domestic businesses as UK consumers can purchase cheaper alternatives from the USA.

    C – It is more expensive for travellers from the USA to visit the UK.

    D – A UK exporter to the USA will benefit because UK exports will be cheaper for Americans to purchase.

2.  A business has purchased some land in unspoilt countryside to build a new factory.

    Which **one** of the following stakeholder groups is most likely to be in conflict with the business?  [1]

    A – Pressure groups

    B – Shareholders

    D – Suppliers

    C – Workers

3.  Explain **one** benefit that technology can have on the costs of a business.  [3]

4.  Explain **one** advantage to a business of complying with consumer law.  [3]

5.  Explain **one** impact on a business of rising inflation.  [3]

6.  Discuss the impact on a business of falling interest rates.  [6]

**For the following questions you must refer to the case study on the previous page.**

7.  If the price of a room at the *Waveney House Hotel* is £110, and the exchange rate was £1 = €1.2, calculate how much would it cost a European tourist to stay in euros. You are advised to show your working.  [2]

8.  Outline **one** way a weakening of the UK pound (£) may impact on the *Waveney House Hotel*.  [2]

9.  Analyse the impact the *Waveney House Hotel* may have on the local community.  [6]

10. Analyse the impact that new technology has had on the *Waveney House Hotel*.  [6]

11. Evaluate whether changes in the economic climate are the greatest external influence on the *Waveney House Hotel*.

    You should use the information provided as well as your knowledge of business.  [12]

# TOPICS FOR THEME 2
## BUILDING A BUSINESS 1BS0/02

## Information about Paper 2

**Written exam: 1 hour 30 minutes**
**90 marks**
**All questions are mandatory**
**50% of qualification grade**
**Calculators are permitted in this examination.**

**Specification coverage**

Growing the business, making marketing decisions,
making operational decisions, making financial decisions,
making human resource decisions.

The content for this assessment will be drawn from topics 2.1 to 2.5 in
the specification.

**Assessment overview**

The paper is divided into three sections:
Section A: 35 marks
Section B: 30 marks
Section C: 25 marks.

The paper will consist of calculations, multiple-choice, short-answer
and extended-writing questions. Questions in Sections B and C will
be based on business contexts given in the paper.

# BUSINESS GROWTH

After surviving the initial years and becoming established, a business may want to grow. The owners will have to make a decision as to whether they grow internally or externally. As businesses become larger, they may even want to become a public limited company.

## Internal growth

**Internal growth** is characterised by a business that grows naturally by gradually increasing the number of products that it sells. It is also called **organic growth**. Firms can achieve internal growth through the following methods:

**New products:** Businesses can grow by introducing **new products** onto the market. Conducting research and development into new ideas, adopting **new technology** and being innovative will help a business achieve this.

**New markets:** A business can grow by selling its existing products in **new markets**. This is achieved by adapting the **marketing mix**, for instance they could aim at a different target market by changing the price or the way a product is promoted. A business could also look to sell its products in new **overseas markets**, whether that is by physically locating in foreign countries or by using e-commerce.

## External growth

**External growth** happens when a business grows by joining with another business, whether that be by a merger or a takeover. It is also known as **inorganic growth**.

**Merger:** A merger is where two or more businesses agree to join together to share resources.

**Takeover:** A takeover is where one business buys a majority shareholding in another.

### Benefits of external growth

Demand will be increasing so this could be the right time to invest and grow the business. Therefore, a business may find:

➕ Growth can be quicker than internal growth.

➕ Combined business benefits from shared resources and skills.

### Drawbacks of external growth

➖ Difficult to integrate two businesses together.

➖ It can be an expensive process.

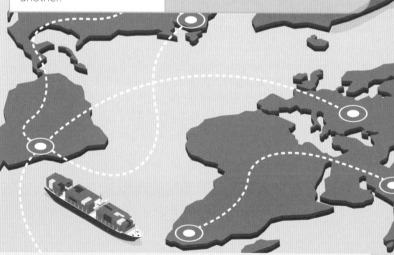

Discuss the impact on a business of growing internally. [3]

*One impact is that growth is slower than growing externally[M]. This is because to grow you have to convince more customers to buy the product which takes time[M], therefore revenues and profits increase at a slower rate[M].*

*A second impact is that internal growth is cheaper than external growth[M]. This is because the business is growing gradually[M]. This enables the business to keep costs low[M] allowing them to be more competitive in the market[M]. This helps the growth to be successful.*

# FINANCING GROWTH

To grow a business costs money, whether it is to purchase another business or to fund research and development needed for internal growth. There are a number of funding options available for growing a business. These can be self-generated or obtained from sources outside the business.

## Internal sources of finance

**Retained profit** is profit that a business has generated that it can reinvest in itself. This source is cheaper than other methods and it allows the owners to maintain their control. However, once it is used, the business will not be able to use it for other projects. Whether it is suitable may be dependent on how much profit the business generates.

**Selling assets**, for example machinery, buildings or intellectual property, can generate finance for a business. A business may raise funds in this way as it is cheap - no repayments are necessary. The drawback of this option is that once sold, the business will not be able to use the assets. Whether selling assets is appropriate may be dependent on how much the assets are required.

## External sources of finance

**Loan capital** is funding borrowed from financial institutions.

**Share capital** is raised by issuing or selling shares in a business. One benefit is that large amounts of funds can be sourced, while also keeping ongoing costs to a minimum as no repayments are made. However, depending on how many shares are given away, it could mean that the owners lose control. This is particularly true if the business goes through flotation and becomes a **plc**.

Discuss the impact on a business of financing growth using loan capital. [6]

*One impact is that the owners will maintain control of the business[✓]. This is because the bank will not take a controlling interest[✓]. This will allow the original owners to continue to make all the decisions[✓], allowing the business to be run with the original owners' values[✓].*

*A second impact is that loan capital is more expensive than some sources[✓]. This is because the business will have to make repayments which will include interest payments[✓]. This increases fixed costs[✓] and therefore also increases total costs[✓], making it harder to make a profit[✓].*

## Public limited companies (plc)

Growing businesses may decide to change their ownership and become a **public limited company (plc)**. A **plc** is an incorporated business that can access huge financial resources by selling shares on a stock exchange. This is achieved through **flotation**.

**Benefits**
- Can raise finance by selling shares.
- The shareholders have limited liability.
- Public are more aware of the business.
- Public perceive them as more reliable.

**Drawbacks**
- A plc is at risk from potential takeovers.
- There will be increased media attention.
- Financial accounts are available for public viewing.
- Potential loss of control after flotation.

# CHANGES IN BUSINESS AIMS AND OBJECTIVES

As businesses grow, what they aim to achieve may need adapting. A well-established firm that is experiencing high demand, may no longer need survival as its main objective, but may wish to aim for growth. Many factors affect the aims and objectives that a business will pursue.

## Why businesses objectives change

### Market conditions

The level of economic activity will impact a business' aim. When consumers have lots of disposable income and demand is high, a business may have new opportunities to seek growth.

### Legislation

New regulation may impact the aims and objectives of a business as it may affect the products and services that the business offers.

## Technology

A business' aim may have to change due to changes in technology. Technology may allow for new and improved inventions to be designed and manufactured. Spending money in this area may be more important than growth, particularly if competitors are taking advantage of it.

### Internal reasons

There are many factors from inside a business that may cause it to change its aims and objectives. One example is that they could have new owners or managers who have a different vision for the business.

Explain **one** reason why the performance of a business can impact its aims and objectives.  [3]

*If a business is performing really well then it may want to follow an objective of growth[1]. This is because its current output may not be enough to meet the demand for the product[1], therefore by growing, they can increase capacity and makes more sales[1].*

## How business aims and objectives change as business evolves

Businesses that are performing well may have the following objectives:
- Growth
- Entering new markets
- Growing the workforce
- Increasing the product range

Businesses that are not performing so well, may pursue the following objectives (which may involve downsizing):
- Focus on survival
- Exiting markets
- Reducing the size of the workforce
- Decreasing the product range

# BUSINESS AND GLOBALISATION

**Globalisation** is the expansion of trade by businesses to operate internationally across many different countries. It is having an increasing impact on how businesses operate as more compete internationally. Governments take action to ensure that domestic firms are protected.

## The impact of globalisation on businesses

**Imports:** The goods and services brought into one country from another. The rise of globalisation has meant that consumers can now buy goods from foreign companies more easily. This means that UK firms will face more competition, making it harder to survive.

**Exports:** The goods and services produced in one country and sold to another. The rise of globalisation has opened up new markets for UK businesses to sell their products to. This has given businesses opportunities to grow and potentially increase their profits.

**Business location:** Globalisation has allowed businesses to more easily locate overseas. By doing so, they may be able to benefit from cheaper labour, allowing them to reduce their costs. This would make them more competitive.

**Multinationals:** A business that operates in multiple countries. These large businesses benefit from lower costs of production and from the fact that they have physical locations near their customers in the countries that they operate in. Other businesses must adapt in order to compete with a multinational.

1. Explain **one** benefit to UK businesses from the rise in the number of imports entering the UK. [3]

*One benefit is that UK manufacturers can import cheaper raw materials from abroad[1]. This reduces the total cost of production[1], allowing the business to sell the products at a lower price or to have an increased profit margin[1].*

*UK businesses may now be able to import products for resale that they may not have been able to get a hold of before[1]. This could cause more customers to be attracted to the business[1]. This could lead to increased revenues and profits[1].*

2. Explain **one** drawback to a multinational of setting up a location in a foreign country. [3]

*One drawback is that a business may not fully understand the needs of the customers in the country where they are choosing to set up[1]. As a result, the product may not be suitable if they do not adapt it[1], meaning that customers may not buy the product and the business could get into financial trouble[1].*

*One drawback is that health and safety regulations may be different[1]. This could mean that the business' product needs to be adapted to fit with the country's regulations[1]. As a result, costs could increase[1] making the products less competitive in the new market[1].*

# BARRIERS TO INTERNATIONAL TRADE

A **trade barrier** is a measure taken by the government of a country to protect domestic firms from foreign competition.

### Tariff

A **tariff** is a tax that governments place on goods imported into the country. This will mean that it is more expensive to buy an imported good than a domestic equivalent.

### Trade bloc

A **trade bloc** is an agreement between a set of countries to have free trade between them. This means that no barriers to trade will be enforced when buying or selling goods across borders within the bloc. Any business who is from a country outside the bloc may be subject to trade barriers.

You won't be asked to name specific trading blocs that exist in the world, although it may be useful to know what they are and how they operate.

One example is ASEAN (Association of Southeast Asian Nations).

## How businesses compete internationally

Developments in the **Internet** and the use of **e-commerce** have allowed businesses to sell their products and services to global website users. This has allowed businesses to enter foreign markets without the need for expensive physical locations or distribution networks. This allows them to keep costs down so they can remain competitively priced.

To successfully compete on an international scale, businesses may need to adapt their marketing mix so that they meet the needs of consumers in foreign markets.

Businesses that are not performing so well may pursue the following objectives (which may involve downsizing):

### Product

Businesses may need to adapt their products to meet the needs of the customers. Cultures, tastes and fashions may be very different to their home county.

Legislation may be different, therefore products must meet the required safety regulations.

### Price

Businesses may need to reduce their prices in order to compete with increased competition and to match the expectations of the consumers.

Price may have to take into account any tariffs that are charged.

### Promotion

Promotion must be adapted to the local culture and abide by local legislation.

### Place

Businesses may have to look at where their products are traditionally sold and may need to find locations that match this. This may include being located online.

# ETHICS, THE ENVIRONMENT AND BUSINESS

As society becomes more aware of ethical and environmental issues, there is growing pressure on businesses to behave responsibly. Although this brings many benefits, it involves a trade-off with profit that may have a negative impact on financial performance.

Business **ethics** involves placing moral values above making profits. There is also a trade-off between profit and being environmentally responsible.

## Ethical and environmental considerations, and the profit trade-off

- A business may choose to pay workers a fair wage rather than exploiting them.
- A business may choose to pay suppliers a fair amount for their materials.
- A business may choose to invest in **renewable energy**.
- A business may choose to source resources ethically.
- A business may choose to be honest and treat customers fairly.
- A business may use locally sourced materials rather than purchasing from afar, thus reducing its **product miles** and **carbon footprint**.
- A business may use biodegradable packaging rather than single-use plastics.
- A business may choose to ensure that it cleans up all its waste rather than dumping it.
- A business may choose to be more **sustainable**.

All these examples are of ethical and responsible attitudes towards the environment, but they all involve additional expenditure. This may mean that a business does not make as much profit as it could have done, had it chosen not to behave so responsibly. That is the trade-off a business must accept.

Explain **one** benefit to a business of acting in an ethical manner. [3]

*One benefit is that the business may gain a reputation for being an ethically minded company[1]. As a result, customers will think more highly of the business and may choose to shop there[1]. This could potentially increase sales and profits[1].*

## The impact of pressure groups

A **pressure group** is an organisation that aims to highlight certain issues in order to get governments and businesses to change their behaviour. They achieve this by lobbying officials and staging protests to influence a firm's marketing mix:

- **Product** – They want ethically produced and environmentally friendly products.
- **Price** – They want businesses to pay fair wages and a fair amount for supplies.
- **Place** – They want a business not to exploit its location and to use locally sourced materials.
- **Promotion** – They want businesses to provide accurate information.

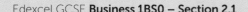

## CASE STUDY

*Marks & Spencer (M&S) plc* is a multinational retailer with strong roots and headquarters in the UK. They sell quality home, clothing and food products, the majority of which is *M&S*'s own brand. They employ 78,000 people and have more than 1,500 stores across 57 countries. This is an area for further potential growth for the business as they look to increase their international offering. Their objective is to create a much more competitive, localised version of *M&S* in those selected markets where they can attain a sustainable market share.

*M&S* have a reputation of being an ethical and environmentally conscious organisation, having previously been named in Forbes' list of the world's most ethical companies. They achieved this through the implementation of their Plan A. Plan A is a multi-year sustainability transformation plan that is regularly updated to reflect the risks and opportunities that social and environmental issues pose for the business. By committing to this plan, they have achieved the following:

- Reduced carrier bag usage by 90%
- They were the world's first retailer to become carbon neutral
- They use 100% responsibly sourced wood in their furniture

In a recent report on Plan A, *M&S* is focusing on three areas:

**People:** *M&S* want all the people working in their business and in their supply chain to have a voice and to receive a fair wage for their work.

**Product:** They state that they source their products responsibly, working closely with suppliers to ensure high standards. They also ensure that no food or clothing goes to waste.

**Planet:** As a business, *M&S* are driving down their gas emissions. They are engaging with the campaign against single use plastic, stating that they have a commitment to reduce waste whilst also reusing and recycling packaging. They are committed to becoming a zero-waste business.

*M&S* have been recognised by various bodies for their efforts in being ethical and sustainable, receiving a number of awards. They received an award from The Climate Change Coalition (2019 Large Business Award) and the Corporate Human Rights Benchmark Award (2019 second retailer in Apparel & Agriculture). Despite all this, *M&S* reported a fall in profit before tax by 20.2% from £84.2m (30th March 2019) to £67.2m in the year ended 28th March 2020.

50  ClearRevise

# EXAMINATION PRACTICE

1.  Which **one** of the following may be an objective of a business that is performing well?           [1]

    A – The business may be looking to decrease the product range.

    B – The business may look to achieve enough sales to break even.

    C – The business may look to grow by entering new markets.

    D – The business may want to exit markets.

2.  Which **one** of the following is an example of a business behaving in an environmentally friendly way?           [1]

    A – The business may use a lot of non-renewable energies.

    B – The business recycles all waste.

    C – The business uses materials transported from countries all over the world.

    D – The business uses plastic packaging rather than paper.

3.  Give **one** reason why a business may have to change its objective.           [1]

4.  Explain **one** drawback to a business of growing via a takeover.           [3]

5.  Explain **one** drawback to a business of financing growth by selling assets.           [3]

6.  Explain **one** impact of globalisation on a business.           [3]

7.  Discuss the impact on a business of becoming a public limited company (plc).           [6]

**For the following questions you must refer to the case study on the previous page.**

8.  Outline **one** benefit to *M&S* of the UK government imposing a tariff on imports.           [2]

9.  Outline **one** method *M&S* use to compete internationally.           [2]

10. *M&S* are looking to finance their future growth through **one** of the following options:

    • Option 1: Retained profit.

    • Option 2: Issuing share capital.

    Justify which of the **two** options you think *M&S* should use to finance their growth.           [9]

11. Evaluate the importance to *M&S* of being ethically responsible.

    You should use the information provided as well as your knowledge of business.           [12]

# PRODUCT

Product is one of the four elements that make up the marketing mix. A business must ensure that they have a **design mix** that enables a product to be differentiated from others in the market.

## The design mix

The design mix of a product is made up of three elements:

**Function:** What is the purpose of the product? Does the product perform as it should?

**Cost:** The cost of the product will be very closely linked to the price charged to customers. To be competitive, businesses must try to keep costs minimised so a lower price can be charged.

**Aesthetics:** A product's appearance is important to customers. A product that is pleasing to the eye may have a better chance of being sold.

An evaluation question may ask you to evaluate which of the elements of the **design mix** is most important. A good conclusion will recognise that a business needs to consider all elements to be successful. For instance, if you have a product that functions well and looks amazing but costs so much to make, it may mean the price that needs to be charged to make a profit is not feasible. However, in the exam, decide which of the elements might have slightly more importance. This will be the area that allows the product to be different. Use the case study to help with this.

## The importance of differentiation

A business must **differentiate** its product to be successful in the market. This means making a product distinctive in some way when compared with rival products.

By differentiating a product, a business is able to charge a higher price, potentially leading to increased profits. Other ways of differentiating a product or service include:

- Branding
- Being cheaper than others
- Having better customer service
- A better functioning product
- Better quality or durability
- Better recyclability or ecological friendliness
- Having a wider product range

Explain **one** method a business could use to differentiate itself from rivals. [3]

*One method is by making their product look different to others[1]. This could be by using bright colours or having a unique design[1]. As a result, the product would be eye catching to consumers and really stand out from competing products[1].*

# THE PRODUCT LIFE CYCLE

Every product has a life span. To ensure a business continues to be successful it needs to understand the life cycle of its products. If it believes that the sales of a product may soon start to fall, the business can take some actions to extend its life span.

## The phases of the product life cycle

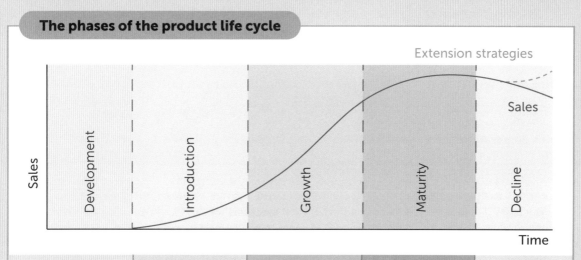

| Development | Introduction | Growth | Maturity | Decline |
|---|---|---|---|---|
| Research and development is employed to come up with a marketable product. As this is pre-launch, no sales are made, but the business incurs lots of costs, so related cash-flow is negative. | The product is launched onto the market. Sales start to increase. Cash-flow is likely to remain negative as the business must heavily promote the product to develop awareness of it. | Sales will start to rise more rapidly after a successful launch as customers become more familiar with the product. As sales start to rise, cash-flow starts to become positive. | Sales levels and cash-flow are at their highest. However, growth in sales will start to slow down. The market may become saturated as more competitors enter the market. | Sales of the product decrease. This may be because the product is outdated. If this continues, the business may decide to withdraw the product. |

## Extension strategies

Before a business' product enters the decline phase, a business can use an **extension strategy** to extend the maturity phase of the life cycle. It can do this by:

- Targeting a new market segment or new market
- Increasing the usage amongst existing customers
- Modifying the product
- Changing the image of the product
- Increasing promotion through advertising or price offers

# PRICE

The price a business charges plays an important role in developing a successful marketing mix. A business must choose which pricing strategy to adopt, but there are many factors that will influence this decision.

## Pricing strategies

A business must position their products using a pricing strategy scale between a high price (**price skimming**) or a low price (**price penetration**).

**Price skimming:** A business will set a high price for its product as it is launched into the market. This may be because it is a technologically superior product, of higher quality than the rest of the market or is highly differentiated in some way, meaning people are prepared to pay more for it.

**Price penetration:** A business will sell a product at a low price. This may be how they are differentiating their product. It is likely that this strategy will be used in the mass market with the aim to sell higher volumes to a greater proportion of the total market.

Whether a business adopts a high or low price strategy, they must consider the costs of making the product. Without knowing what it costs to make a product, they will not know if they are making any profit on each sale. In competitive markets, a business must know what competitors are charging for similar products or services.

## Influences on the pricing strategies

**Technology:** New technology in the production process can help to lower a business' costs, therefore a lower price can be charged.

**Competition:** As competition increases it may mean that a more competitive price has to be charged unless the business is highly differentiated in terms of brand name and quality.

**Market segments:** A business will have to adopt a different strategy depending on the market segment targeted. In doing so, the ability of that segment to pay for the products must be considered.

**Product life cycle:** The phase that the product is in will determine whether a higher or lower price can be charged. For instance, when the product is in the decline phase, charging a low price may encourage customers to purchase it.

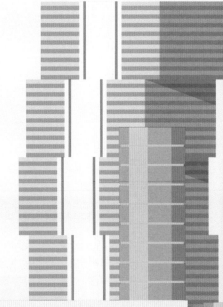

Explain **one** reason why a business may need to know what price competitors are charging. [3]

*It is important because a business may have a similar product to its rivals[1]. If they charged a much higher price, they may not receive many sales[1]. Consequently, this could lead to the business not selling enough products to breakeven[1].*

# PROMOTION

What brands do you want to be associated with? Why? What have these companies done to make you feel this way?

Promotion helps to create awareness of a business and its products. Its purpose is to instil the desire in a customer to want to purchase the product or to be associated with a brand by building a strong brand image.

## Promotion strategies

### Advertising

Communication is used to inform potential customers about products and to persuade them to buy. It can take many forms: TV, print media, websites and social media.

**Benefit**
+ Can reach a large potential audience. Particularly effective for older generations.

**Drawback**
− Can be expensive, especially if people ignore adverts, or watch TV on demand.

## Sponsorship

A method of raising awareness of a business' brand name in return for financial support of events or public spaces. For example, these events could be cultural, sporting or musical.

**Benefit**
+ Can provide a lot of brand exposure. Particularly effective when targeting events for different market segments.

**Drawback**
− If the event being sponsored gets bad publicity, the business' image may suffer. It can also be expensive.

### Special offers

Special offers commonly include 'Buy one get one free', refer-a-friend campaigns, or discounts off the full price.

**Benefit**
+ Customers feel they are getting a bargain.

**Drawback**
− Profit margins will be reduced.

### Product trials

A business will offer free samples to potential customers so that they can try the product before they buy it.

**Benefit**
+ Encourages customers to try a new product.

**Drawback**
− Can be costly to give away free samples.

### Branding

The creation of an identity that distinguishes the business from that of rival firms.

**Benefit**
+ Can add value to a product and will develop loyalty and repeat purchases.

**Drawback**
− Can take a long time to develop a strong brand.

Explain **one** benefit to a business of viral advertising. [3]

*If a business can use social media to make an advert go viral, many consumers will share it[1]. This means that the business will gain a lot of exposure[1], which potentially could lead to increased sales[1].*

## Use of technology in promotion

Businesses are now making more use of technology in their promotional strategies. **E-newsletters** and the use of **social media** have become much more common. **Targeted advertising**, particularly using pay-per-click social media and search engine marketing (based on related keyword searches), is also heavily used.

# PLACE

Place considers a business' location and the method of distribution used. This determines how the product gets to the end consumer.

## Methods of distribution

A **distribution channel** is the route that a product takes from where it is manufactured to where it is sold to the end consumer. This could be direct or could involve the use of a retailer.

### Direct

Direct distribution is employed by businesses who sell their product directly to the customer. This allows the producer to engage in communication with the customer so they will know if there is a problem. It also allows them to know what the needs of the customers are, so they can easily adapt their product if needed. Many e-commerce businesses will sell directly to customers via their own website.

### E-tailer

An **e-tailer** is an online retailer. They buy and sell goods on the Internet. Some businesses may be a retailer and an e-tailer having both physical stores and online platforms.

### Retailer

Some manufacturers will sell their products to a **retailer**. A retailer acts as a 'middle-man' who buys products from a producer in larger quantities and then sells them on for a higher price to the end consumer. The retailer is usually more convenient for a customer to visit and buy from.

1. Explain **one** benefit to a business of using a retailer to distribute their products. [3]

   *One benefit is that customers can see the products and potentially try them[1]. This will give the customers confidence that they are buying the right product[1]. Therefore, the business may make more sales than they would if they were selling them directly[1].*

2. Discuss the benefit of e-tailing to a business. [6]

   *One advantage is that an e-tailer can sell to a global market[✓]. This is because they are selling goods on the Internet[✓]. This may enable them to reach many more customers than if they used physical stores[✓]. This could lead to increased sales and revenue[✓].*

   *Another advantage is that they do not need expensive retail locations[✓]. This may lead to lower fixed costs since they do not need to pay to open physical stores[✓]. This would mean that total costs may be lower[✓] which would allow them to sell their products for less[✓].*

# USING THE MARKETING MIX TO MAKE BUSINESS DECISIONS

For a business to be successful, it needs to develop an integrated marketing mix as this will have an influence on a business' competitive advantage. Each of the elements is inter-related and must complement each other.

## Influence of the elements

All the elements of the marketing mix will influence each other. If a business decides to produce a new, high-quality, luxury and innovative product utilising the latest technology, the product will influence the other factors in the following ways:

**Price:** The product is likely to cost a lot to manufacture and the price will need to be set high to reflect this and provide a satisfactory margin.

**Promotion:** The promotion strategies used must be appropriate given the product is of a high quality and likely to be targeted at the premium market.

**Place:** To uphold the product's superior image it must be sold in suitable establishments that enhance this image. Distribution is not likely to be extensive in order to protect the luxury image.

Explain **one** way that promotion may impact on the price element of the marketing mix. [3]

*A business may decide to conduct free promotion using regular posts on social media rather than using TV advertising[1]. This will mean that the overall costs of the business are lower[1]. This will mean that the business can charge a lower price for its product[1].*

*A promotional campaign may be trying to portray an image of luxury[1] and the price of the product needs to reflect this[1]. Consequently, the business may use a price skimming strategy[1].*

## The marketing mix and competitive advantage

**Competitive advantage** is a gain that a business has over its rivals in the market. Each of the elements of the marketing mix can help to build that competitive advantage and give a reason for a customer to buy the product of one business over another.

- A product can have unique features and be of a superior quality when compared to similar competitor products.
- A business may be able to produce their product for a lower cost than any of their rivals. Therefore, they can sell it to customers for less.
- A business may have a very eye-catching advertising campaign that could become viral and is seen by a wide audience, leading to the business building a strong brand.
- A business may have a wide distribution network meaning that their products are sold in more outlets than competitor products, allowing a business to gain more exposure.

# CASE STUDY

**ASOS plc** is a British online fashion and cosmetic retailer who aim their products at young adults. They sell over 850 brands via their website as well as selling their own range of clothing and accessories, shipping products to 196 countries. They recognise that each individual is unique so to help customers find the right fit for them, they offer their brand of clothing in 30 different sizes all at the same price. In 2019 they had 2.3bn visits to their platforms with 20.3m active customers.

The e-tailer uses digital marketing extensively and to great success. They have attributed nearly 10% of sales to their email marketing strategy. They launched a campaign that took full advantage of the 'Instagram Stories' feature, encouraging customers to upload videos of themselves in clothes purchased from the business. Over 3 million people interacted with the video in the UK and they have widely promoted the #AsSeenOnMe hashtag. In 2018 they also launched an app that allowed users to upload images of clothing they like in order to receive suggestions of matching or similar items that the business stocks.

In 2020 *ASOS* trialled the launch of a new tool on its website that allowed shoppers to see what clothing selections would look like on different body types. It provides online shoppers with a simulated view of what an item of clothing would look like on people of various shapes and sizes, in order to better reflect the body types of individual customers. This helps them to see what it would look like on themselves, before purchasing.

*ASOS* undertakes this innovative approach as the fashion retail market is very competitive. There are many other stores in the market and *ASOS* faces strong competition online from retailers such as Next, boohoo and Prettylittlething.

# EXAMINATION PRACTICE

1.  Which **one** of the following is part of the design mix?                                          [1]
    A – Cost
    B – Growth
    C – Profit
    D – Revenue

2.  In which stage of the product life cycle is cash flow least likely to be negative?                 [1]
    A – Decline
    B – Development
    C – Introduction
    D – Maturity

3.  Explain **one** benefit to a business of knowing which stage of the life cycle its product is in.  [3]

4.  Explain **one** reason why a business may use a high price strategy when launching a new product.  [3]

5.  Discuss the impact on a business of using sponsorship as a promotional strategy.                    [6]

**For the following questions you must refer to the case study on the previous page.**

6.  Outline **one** method that *ASOS* uses to differentiate its products.                              [2]

7.  Outline **one** method *ASOS* may use to extend the life cycle of its products.                     [2]

8.  Analyse the reasons why the design mix of its own brand products is important to *ASOS*.            [6]

9.  Analyse the influence on *ASOS*'s pricing strategy.                                                 [6]

10. Evaluate whether promotion is the biggest source of competitive advantage for *ASOS*.
    You should use the information provided as well as your knowledge of business.                      [12]

# BUSINESS OPERATIONS

It is the purpose of the operations function within a business to produce goods and provide services to the customers. Products can be produced in a variety of ways and a business must choose which method is most suitable for them.

## Methods of production

### Job production

Job production involves the manufacture of a single, unique product made to the specific requirements of the customer. An example of this would be the production of a sports stadium or the making of a bespoke wedding dress.

**Benefit**
- Meets customers' exact requirements.
- High profit margins.
- Usually high quality.

**Drawback**
- High unit costs, so a high price is set.
- Skilled workforce required.
- Can take a longer time to produce, so productivity is low.

### Batch production

Batch production is used to make sets of identical products in batches. Once one batch has been produced, modifications are made to the production process so that a batch of different products can be produced. Examples include the production of bread or furniture.

**Benefit**
- Faster than job production so it has higher productivity than job production.
- Some flexibility as modifications to the process can be made.

**Drawback**
- Time is needed to make modifications between batches.
- There is a greater cost per item than with flow production.

### Flow production

Flow production is also known as mass production and involves production of products along a production line, often using robotics. The products will be identical and manufactured in large quantities. Examples include the production of chocolate bars and glass bottles.

**Benefit**
- Low average unit costs.
- Fast / high production.
- Use of robotics allows for 24/7 manufacture.

**Drawback**
- Expensive to set up due to the cost of machinery.
- Repetitive work is demotivating for workers.
- A breakdown on the production line halts all production.

## Impact of technology on production

Technology has helped to increase productivity with more consistent quality. Products are made with fewer employees and in a shorter time frame. Although expensive to set up initially, average costs of production are reduced long term, allowing a business to be more price competitive. Production is also more flexible as technology has enabled design modifications to be much easier through the use of **Computer Aided Design (CAD)** and **Computer Aided Manufacture (CAM)**.

Explain **one** way that technology has impacted on the quality of a business' product. [3]

*One way is that identical products are produced[1]. This is because robotics used can manufacture products with extreme precision and to set specifications[1], thus there may be fewer defects[1].*

# BAR GATE STOCK GRAPHS

Managing stock involves organising the raw materials that are used in production, work-in-progress and finished goods that are waiting to be sold. A business must decide what is the most efficient and reliable method of stock control as well as which suppliers to use.

## Bar gate stock graphs

A **bar gate stock graph** is a diagrammatical way of managing stock. It helps a business to know when more stock should be ordered.

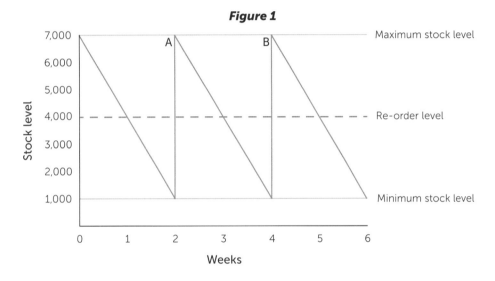

**Figure 1**

### Maximum stock level

The total amount of stock that a business can hold at one time, in this case it is 7000 units.

### Minimum stock level

Also known as **buffer stock**. It is the lowest amount of stock that a business should hold. This allows a business to still produce goods should there be a delay in delivery. In this case it is 1000 units.

### Re-order level

This is the point at which new stock will be ordered. In this case stock will be ordered when there are 4000 units remaining. This provides sufficient stock levels during the stock lead time.

### Lead time

The time that it takes for new stock to arrive once ordered. In this case it is 1 week.

---

Calculate the size of delivery A in *Figure 1*.                                     [2]

*Stock level at the point a delivery arrives = 1000 units. Stock level after delivery = 7000 units.*

*7000 − 1000[1] = Amount of stock ordered = 6000 units[2].*

# WORKING WITH SUPPLIERS

## Procurement

**Procurement** is the term used to describe the process a business goes through in finding and obtaining the right materials and supplies to be used in the production process. If a business can find the right supplier then the process can become more efficient. Effective procurement will result in finding a supplier that:

- Will supply the best **quality** materials at the best possible price.
- Will be **flexible**, **quick** and **reliable** in delivery so that the business gets the right supplies at the right time, avoiding stoppages in production or sales.
- Has the materials that a business needs in **stock**.
- Will negotiate prices so that the business can make **cost** savings, particularly when buying in bulk, or for having a long-standing relationship the business can **trust**.

## Just in time (JIT)

**Just in time** stock control is used by businesses that hold no stock. Raw materials are ordered as they are needed and are used straight away on the production line once they arrive. For this system to work, the business must have a good relationship with its supplier, and a well organised production system so it knows precisely when and what to order.

| Benefits | Drawbacks |
|---|---|
| ⊕ The cost of holding stock is reduced. | ⊖ Will not receive bulk-buying discounts. |
| ⊕ Good cash-flow as money is not tied up in stock. | ⊖ Any delay in delivery may halt production. |
| ⊕ Less chance of stock being damaged, spoiled, stolen or becoming obsolete whilst in storage. | ⊖ The business is less able to meet sudden surges in demand or large one-off orders. |

Discuss the impact on a business of choosing the wrong raw material suppliers. [6]

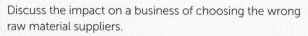

*The services provided by the supplier can directly influence the reputation of a business[✓]. If materials supplied are not of a sufficient quality, it can impact on the quality of the business' products[✓]. This could then lead to dissatisfied customers[✓] who may in turn, give the business negative reviews[✓]. This could lead to the business gaining a poor reputation[✓]. This may adversely affect future sales[✓].*

*There could also be an impact on a business' costs[✓]. This is because a reputable supplier may deliver quality materials, but they may be more expensive than other options[✓]. This would mean that variable costs would increase[✓], meaning that the business would have to increase the price that they charge the customers[✓] in order to maintain profit margins[✓].*

# MANAGING QUALITY

A business' products and services must be of a sufficient quality to satisfy the customer's needs and wants. If quality falls short of these expectations, then the business could suffer as a result. A business can either use a **quality control** or **quality assurance** system.

## Quality control

**Quality control** involves checking the quality of a product at the end of the production line by a team of quality controllers and inspectors. Their job is to ensure that each product or batch meets a specific set of standards before being sold to the customers.

| Benefits | Drawbacks |
|---|---|
| ⊕ Defective products will not make it to market. | ⊖ There can be a lot of waste as defects are only found at the end of the production process. |
| ⊕ The system is not disruptive to workers as quality is inspected at the end of production. | ⊖ This process can be costly, not only in terms of waste, but inspectors have to be paid. |

## Quality assurance

**Quality assurance** requires each individual worker to be responsible for the quality of their own work.

Quality is a focus at every stage of the production process. As such it aims to prevent errors from being made in the first place.

| Benefits | Drawbacks |
|---|---|
| ⊕ Can be motivating to staff as they have more responsibility. | ⊖ Production may be more time consuming as each worker checks their own quality. |
| ⊕ In theory there should be no wastage as errors are rectified immediately before the products move along the production line. | ⊖ Staff may need training to take on the extra responsibility. |

Discuss the benefit to a business of producing a high-quality product. [6]

*One benefit is that it can provide a competitive advantage[✓]. This is because customers may see the product as superior compared to competitor products[✓]. As a result, they may be more likely to purchase the product from the business[✓], possibly for a higher price too, leading to increased revenue and potentially profit[✓].*

*A second benefit is that controlling quality can reduce costs[✓]. This is because there will be fewer defect products[✓], meaning that the business will have less wastage[✓]. This leads to the business being more efficient[✓].*

# THE SALES PROCESS

Offering good customer service is one way that a business can gain an advantage over competitors. By looking after customers, a business will gain a good reputation that will help them to be successful.

Good service throughout the sales process involves the following:

## Product knowledge

Being able to answer customer questions will help them determine which product or service is most suitable for fulfilling their needs. It will make a customer feel more confident when purchasing from a business that really understands what it offers.

## Responses to customer feedback

Receiving feedback is a good way for a business to interact with customers, as long as they act upon any feedback received, whether it is positive or negative. If it is negative, this needs to be handled with sensitivity so that the situation can be resolved. That way the business may retain the custom in the future.

## Customer engagement

Any interaction between the customer and the business needs to be positive in order to make them want to engage with the business more. Making the customer feel valued will enhance their experience and ensure that they know that the business cares about them.

## Speed and efficiency of service

Dealing with customers promptly and shipping the product to them in a timely fashion will help a business make customers happy. A customer is more likely to make a purchase if the sales process is quick and easy.

## Post-sales service

The customer's experience with a business does not finish when they purchase the product. For some businesses, the service the customer receives afterwards is just as important.

Explain **one** benefit to a business of providing good customer service. [3]

*Good customer service will lead to satisfied and loyal customers as they feel that the business really values them[1]. As a result, they are more likely to undertake repeat purchases[1], or leave favourable online reviews of their experience[1], which could lead to an increase in reputation[1], and potentially sales and revenue of the business[1].*

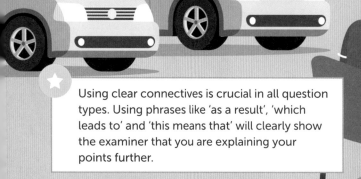

Using clear connectives is crucial in all question types. Using phrases like 'as a result', 'which leads to' and 'this means that' will clearly show the examiner that you are explaining your points further.

# CASE STUDY

*Toyota* is a multinational vehicle manufacturer selling its vehicles in more than 170 countries across the globe. One of their most popular models is the *Toyota* Corolla, which has sold over 43 million models over the years. One of the reasons for the continued success of the Corolla is its quality. The car has a great reputation for reliability with many generations. It also offers good levels of comfort at affordable prices.

For many years, *Toyota* has taken the lead in efficient manufacturing techniques. Their objective is to manufacture vehicles in the quickest and most efficient way so that they can deliver them to the customer as swiftly as possible.

In order to improve efficiencies, *Toyota* adopts a just in time approach to stock control. The assembly line is only stocked with the required number of necessary materials that will be used in immediate production. The management of *Toyota* recognise that storing large quantities of stock can lead to a lot of waste and storage costs, which will have a negative impact on the vehicle manufacturer's efficiency.

*Toyota* utilises a flow production technique in its factories, making use of large amounts of automation, although the process is overseen by employees. In the production process, the business utilises a system of quality assurance. If there is a problem in the production process that is affecting quality, the machine will come to an immediate halt and the problem will be rectified so that the quality of production is reliable.

These production systems have given *Toyota* a competitive advantage against its rivals such as *Volkswagen*, *Hyundai* and *General Motors*. They have enabled it to become one of the biggest vehicle manufacturers in the world, selling nearly 9 million vehicles in the last year.

# EXAMINATION PRACTICE

1. Which **one** of the following is a benefit of batch production? [1]

   A – All the products made will be identical.

   B – It is the production method with the lowest average costs per unit.

   C – Products produced are unique to each customer.

   D – Productivity is higher than that of job production.

2. Using the bar stock graph in Figure 1, calculate:

   a) The size of order A in units. You are advised to show your workings. [2]

   b) The lead time for order B. You are advised to show your workings. [2]

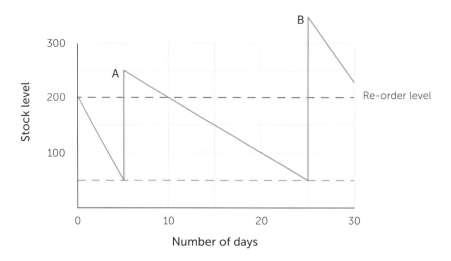

3. Explain **one** benefit to a business of using job production. [3]

4. Explain **one** benefit to a business of holding large stock levels. [3]

5. Explain **one** benefit of having staff who have good product knowledge. [3]

**For the following questions you must refer to the case study on the previous page.**

6. Outline **one** benefit that technology has had on *Toyota's* production. [2]

7. Outline **one** reason why choosing the right supplier is important to *Toyota*. [2]

8. Analyse the impact to *Toyota* of using flow production. [6]

9. Analyse the impact to *Toyota* of using a just in time (JIT) system of stock control. [6]

10. Evaluate the importance of *Toyota's* quality assurance system in providing the business with a competitive advantage.

    You should use the information provided as well as your knowledge of business. [12]

# GROSS AND NET PROFIT

There are different measures of profit that a business needs to calculate in order to assess their performance. These are gross profit and net profit. However, to fully assess profitability, a business will also need to calculate and interpret profit margins.

## Calculating gross and net profit

### Gross profit

**Gross profit** is the difference between a business' revenue and the costs associated with making the product, known as the **cost of sales**. Cost of sales includes the cost of raw materials that are directly associated with manufacture or the purchase or products.

**Gross profit = Revenue – Cost of sales**

### Net profit

**Net profit** is the difference between gross profit and operating expenses. Included in operating expenses are the fixed costs not directly associated with making the product. They also include any interest that the business owes on finance borrowed.

**Net profit = Gross profit – Other operating expenses and interest**

## Calculating gross and net profit margin

**Gross profit margin = (Gross profit ÷ Revenue) × 100**
**Net profit margin = (Net profit ÷ Revenue) × 100**

The **gross profit margin** is a measure of how profitable the business is at making and selling the product or service. The **net profit margin** is a test of the overall profitability of the business as it considers all the expenses of the business.

A gross profit of 58.36% means that for every £100 of revenue £58.36 of it is gross profit. A net profit margin of 14.77% means that there is £14.77 of net profit in every £100 of revenue. To assess whether the business has performed better, a business needs to compare these figures with those from recent years and with those of competitor firms.

**Income Statement for ABC plc**

|  | £ |
|---|---|
| Revenue | 95,450 |
| Cost of sales | 39,850 |
| Gross profit | 55,600 |
| Other operating expenses and interest | 41,500 |
| Net profit | 14,100 |

Using the Income Statement for ABC plc, calculate, to two decimal places:
(a) The gross profit margin [2]
(b) The net profit margin [2]

(a) GPM = (55,600 ÷ 95,450) × 100 = **58.25%**

(b) NPM = (14,100 ÷ 95,450) × 100 = **14.77%**

# AVERAGE RATE OF RETURN

A business must often choose between different investment opportunities. For instance, they could have to decide whether to purchase new machinery for its factory or to upgrade its delivery vans. Management will use the average rate of return to help decide which is best.

The **average rate of return (ARR)** is a calculation that allows a business to work out the average yearly profit, as a percentage, of an investment. Businesses will calculate the ARR of different investment projects in order to easily compare the different options.

## Calculating ARR

**ARR = (Average yearly profit ÷ Initial sum invested) × 100**

|  | Project A | Project B |
|---|---|---|
| Average annual profit | £250,000 | £500,000 |
| Initial investment | £800,000 | £3,300,000 |

> In the exam, the examiner is most likely to give you the average yearly profit rather than you having to calculate this.

Calculate, to two decimal places, using the financial information in the table above:
(a) The ARR of project A. [2]
(b) The ARR of project B. [2]

> (a) ARR of project A = (250,000 ÷ 800,000) × 100 = **31.25%**
> (b) ARR of project B = (500,000 ÷ 3,300,000) × 100 = **15.15%**

## Interpreting ARR

ARR is a measure of profitability, so the higher the result, the better. If a project had an ARR of 31.25%, it means that for every £100 invested, the project will yield a yearly profit of £31.25. From this example, it is clear that on financial grounds alone, that Project A would be the better project to invest in as it has a much higher ARR than project B.

> Calculation questions may require you to calculate your answer to 2 decimal places. If this is written in the question, make sure you do as asked. If you write your answer to one decimal place in this situation, you would lose a mark.

# UNDERSTANDING BUSINESS PERFORMANCE

**Quantitative data** is numerical and statistical information that a business can analyse in order to assess its performance. This data comes from a wide variety of sources and is in many forms. Businesses must interpret this data to inform and justify decisions.

## Information from graphs and charts

Using graphs and charts is an easy way for a business to spot trends, relationships or correlation between two sets of data. For example, a business may want to see how their spending on advertising has impacted on their sales figures.

### Marketing data

Data that a business has collected via primary and secondary market research can include customer opinions on a product. This will be used to help adapt the business' marketing mix.

### Market data

This is data about the state of the market that the business operates in. This includes the number of competitors, whether the market is growing or declining, the market share of each firm in the market as well as cost information from different suppliers. This data would help a business to make decisions on issues such as pricing and longer-term strategy.

Explain **one** reason why a business might use financial data. [3]

*A business might use financial data in support of a request for a bank loan[1]. This is because they can use cash-flow forecasts to show that they will have enough money coming in and past financial records to show that they have been successful.[1] This will give the bank confidence that the business will be able to meet the repayments[1].*

### Financial data

This includes financial information about how the business has performed in the past by analysing previous financial accounts and records. These will allow a business to calculate profitability ratios. It also involves looking at future predicted performance using cash-flow forecasts, revenue budgets and cost predictions.

## Limitation of financial information

- Some financial data is historical and there is no guarantee that trends would continue.
- As the data is quantitative, there is no explanation for changes in the data, which may be more important.
- It is not always accurate to compare two sets of data together.
- Data can easily be manipulated and show bias.

When making decisions, a business must also use qualitative data because of these limitations.

# CASE STUDY

*Wagamama Ltd* is a British restaurant chain that serves Asian food based on Japanese cuisine. The first restaurant was opened in Bloomsbury, London back in 1992. As of 2019, the chain boasted a portfolio of 135 directly operated restaurants in the UK. As well as having 135 restaurants they have also set up a delivery kitchen side to their business. *Wagamama* currently operate 'dark kitchens' and are looking to open more. These are kitchens that prepare food at a separate takeaway facility rather than at a restaurant. Customers can order from the usual menu via Deliveroo.

Delivery sales, both from restaurants and 'dark kitchens' rose to 12% of *Wagamama's* total sales in 2019, up from 10% in 2018. This is one of the reasons that the management has identified this as a growth area.

In November 2019, *Wagamama* opened a spin-off restaurant brand called *Mamago* in London. This restaurant produces dishes designed to 'grab and go' in order to meet the needs of a growing number of customers who want food on the go. The chain's famous katsu curry has been adapted into multiple dishes such as katsu chicken wrap, katsu rice bowl and katsu salad.

**Figure 1:** *Wagamama Limited* Income Statement 2018 and 2019

| | £'000s | |
|---|---|---|
| | 2019 | 2018 |
| Revenue | 326,303 | 293,589 |
| Cost of sales | 192,891 | 170,856 |
| Gross profit | 133,412 | 122,733 |
| Other operating expenses and interest | | 97,913 |
| Net profit/(loss) | (24,367)* | 24,820 |

*\* In accounting practice, brackets indicate that a loss has been made.*

**Figure 2:** Share of satisfied customers for casual dining restaurants in the UK by attribute

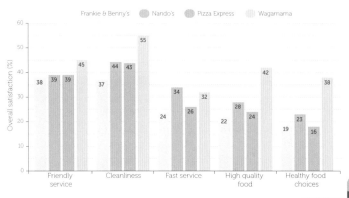

# EXAMINATION PRACTICE

1. Which **one** of the following would be categorised as a piece of market data? [1]

   A – A cash flow forecast.

   B – The budgeted revenues and costs for the coming year.

   C – The number of direct competitors.

   D – The previous year's profit figure.

2. Using the financial information below, which **one** of the following gives the gross profit of the business? [1]

| Revenue | £46,450 |
|---|---|
| Cost of sales | £18,950 |
| Other operating expenses and interest | £22,750 |

   A – £4,750        B – £23,700        C – £27,500        D – £65,400

3. Explain **one** method a business could use to improve its gross profit. [3]

4. Explain **one** way a business may use marketing data. [3]

5. Discuss the limitations to a business of using quantitative data to make decisions. [6]

6. A business is contemplating buying some new machinery. The cost of the machinery is £55,500 and will generate average yearly profits of £7,500.

   Calculate, to 2 decimal places, the average rate of return (ARR) of the machinery purchase. You are advised to show your working. [2]

**For the following questions you must refer to the case study on the previous page.**

7. Using the information in Figure 1, calculate *Wagamama's* other operating expenses and interest in 2019. You are advised to show your working. [2]

8. Calculate, to 2 decimal places, *Wagamama's* gross profit margin for 2019 to 2 decimal places. You are advised to show your working. [2]

9. Calculate, to 2 decimal places, *Wagamama's* net profit margin for 2018 to 2 decimal places. You are advised to show your working. [2]

10. Outline **one** way *Wagamama* could use financial data to help make business decisions. [2]

11. Analyse how *Wagamama* could use the information contained in Figure 2. [6]

12. Evaluate whether opening more *Mamago* restaurants is the most suitable method for *Wagamama* to increase its profit.

    You should use the information provided as well as your knowledge of business. [12]

# ORGANISATIONAL STRUCTURES

An **organisational structure** is the way in which a business is organised in terms of its employees. The structure selected by a business will have an impact on many issues such as employee motivation and communication.

## Hierarchical vs flat structure

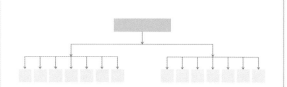

### Hierarchical structure

- Many layers of management.
- Promotional opportunities for staff.
- Managers have a **narrow span of control**.
- Slower communication flow.

### Flat structure

- Shorter **chain of command**.
- Managers have wide spans of control.
- More **delegation** and **authority** given to staff.
- Communication is quicker.

## Centralised vs decentralised structure

### Centralised

A business structure where the main decision-making powers rest with senior management, often based in the business' headquarters. Under this system, all branches of the business will look the same, sell the same products and charge the same amount. The main advantage is that these senior managers have lots of experience in making difficult decisions and the customers know exactly what to expect, regardless of which branch they visit.

### Decentralised

Under this structure, decision making powers are delegated to the local managers. The rationale behind this is that these managers know their local market better than the senior managers. As local employees have the authority to make decisions, they can be made more quickly as approval from those above them in the hierarchy is not needed.

1. Explain **one** drawback to a business of having a decentralised structure. [3]

*The reputation of the firm may be ruined by the actions of one branch[1]. This is because the local managers can make their own decisions on what to sell and how to price it[1]. If they sell a product that is not consistent with the quality of the firm it won't only be that branch that gains a negative image, but the business as a whole[1].*

## Effective communication

If there is effective communication in a business, then everyone is aware of what the business is trying to achieve. Everyone will also know exactly what their role is and what is required of them. Problems can occur in a business if communication is insufficient or excessive. This can have an impact on the motivation of the workforce and efficiency in the following ways:

- Too little communication means that an employee may not understand their role and be demotivated as a result, whilst jobs may not be completed properly.
- Too much communication may cause employees to feel overwhelmed and stressed, whilst also leading to important information being missed or overlooked.

## Barriers to effective communication

### Noise

With noisy distractions, employees may not be able to concentrate fully, causing lower productivity.

### Inappropriate mediums

A telephone call may be an inappropriate medium of communication to explain complicated information which the recipient has to remember.

### Language barriers

For multinationals, having employees that don't speak the same language can be problematic.

### Distance

The physical distance between offices across the globe and in different time zones can make communication ineffective.

### Jargon

The use of technical language can be hard to understand.

### Personalities

Some employees may feel uncomfortable in communicating with other colleagues. This could be because they don't personally like them, or they feel that they cannot approach them. Some employees may simply feel tired or angry which has a negative impact on communication.

2. Explain **one** impact on a business if employees use jargon.                    [3]

*Jargon is a barrier because an employee may not be used to and therefore not understand what is being said[1]. This could cause misinterpretation of the message that is trying to be relayed[1], causing an employee to make errors in the work that they are doing, so productivity falls[1].*

# DIFFERENT WAYS OF WORKING

Many businesses are changing the way they ask employees to work. Flexible working arrangements are much more common, and this can suit both the individual and the business.

## Categories of employment

**Full-time:** Usually classed as someone who works 35 hours a week or more (an individual can not work more than 48 hours per week owing to current regulation).

**Part-time:** Employees that work less than 35 hours per week are classed as part-time, but they have exactly the same rights as a full-time member of staff.

**Flexible hours:** An employee will have to work a certain number of hours a week, but there is flexibility as to when those hours can be completed.

**Zero-hours contract:** Here, there are no guaranteed hours for an employee. When asked, the employee does not have to accept the work offered. This is often used in businesses with large fluctuations in demand.

## Permanent, temporary or freelance

### Permanent

An employee has a contract of employment that has no end date. These can be either full-time or part-time contracts.

**Advantage:** May be more motivated as employees have job security.

**Disadvantage:** Higher costs compared with temporary staff.

### Temporary

A business may employ people for a defined period of time to cover busy periods or staff absence.

**Advantage:** Saves the business money, as they only pay for workers when needed.

**Disadvantage:** Workers may lack experience.

### Freelance

Freelancers are self-employed people who are hired by a business to work on a specific project for a period of time. They are usually highly qualified and can work to a pre-agreed budget.

**Advantage:** Usually experts in their field.

**Disadvantage:** Lack of commitment to a business.

Explain **one** benefit to a business of employing staff using zero-hours contracts. [3]

*One benefit is that it is cheaper for a business[1]. This is because they are only paying for the workers when they are needed[1], as a result money is not wasted, and costs will be minimised allowing the business to remain competitive[1].*

## Impact of technology

Technology has allowed for remote working. Video conferencing, emails and mobile devices can allow employees to communicate and work from home or other locations. This is more efficient for a business as time is saved and expenses are reduced.

# EFFECTIVE RECRUITMENT

There are lots of reasons why a business needs to recruit new workers, from having to replace those who leave, to employing more as the business grows. When recruiting, a business must decide what role is needed and what method they will use to recruit those required.

## Job roles and responsibilities

### Directors

Long-term strategic planning of the business. They discuss and make key decisions faced by the business.

### Senior managers

Senior managers are in control of day-to-day operation and will head up the key functions of the business.

### Supervisors/team leaders

Support and manage the operational staff to ensure that they are completing the tasks of the business.

### Operational staff

Complete the day-to-day operations required for the business to function. Responsible to the supervisors.

### Support staff

Will offer support functions such as looking after a business' IT network or ensuring office spaces are clean.

## Internal / external recruitment

### Internal recruitment

**Internal recruitment**: Vacancies are filled by someone who already works in the business.

- The employee will already know the business.
- It is a faster, easier and cheaper way to recruit.
- Promoting from within can be motivating for employees.

## How businesses recruit people

As part of the recruitment process, a business will produce a **job description** and person specification. A job description is a document telling potential applicants all the details of the job itself including what the main duties are, who the person would report to and what the wage or salary is. A **person specification** is a document that tells applicants about the skills and characteristics that are needed to be able to complete the job. When someone applies for a job, they may also have to send in a **curriculum vitae (CV)** which is a document that tells the business about the education, qualifications and employment history of the applicant.

### External recruitment

**External recruitment**: Businesses employ workers who do not already work for the organisation.

- New employees may bring fresh ideas.
- There may be a bigger pool of potential applicants to choose from.
- External recruitment may be necessary if the vacancy has arisen due to growth of the business.

# EFFECTIVE TRAINING AND DEVELOPMENT

Developing an employee not only benefits the individual, but also has its advantages for the business. Training can take many forms, but it is essential that all businesses conduct ongoing professional development so that employees can keep up to date with the latest industry knowledge and skills.

## Types of training

### Informal training

Training that is usually conducted whilst the employee is undertaking their normal job. It is commonly delivered by other, more experienced, members of staff.

**Benefits**

- ⊕ Training can be tailored to the individual.
- ⊕ It is a cheaper way to train people.

**Drawbacks**

- ⊖ Poor working practices can be passed on.
- ⊖ Having to train whilst undertaking a new job can be stressful.

## Formal training

Training that staff attend in order to improve a specific skill or learn some specific knowledge. Courses are usually conducted away from the individual's normal place of work and led by specialists in that area.

**Benefits**

- ⊕ Training is delivered by specialists.
- ⊕ Usually highly structured and may provide the employee with a qualification.

**Drawbacks**

- ⊖ Attending training courses can be expensive.
- ⊖ Can take employees away from their work.

## Developing employees

As well as training, there are other methods that businesses can use to develop employees. These involve the use of target setting and **performance reviews**.

An employee will have an appraisal with their line manager and agree on some targets that the employee will try to achieve in the coming year.

Training is provided so that the employee gains the skills and knowledge to help them achieve the targets set.

Towards the end of the year, an employee will have a performance review. A supervisor will monitor the employee's progress towards achieving the objectives and then agree a new set for the forthcoming year.

1. Explain **one** benefit to a business of allowing employees to undertake self-learning. [3]

   *Employees can learn at their own pace[1]. Therefore, the employees feel empowered to improve their skills at times convenient to them[1]. As a result, the employees will feel valued as the firms trust them without feeling under pressure to complete courses by a deadline[1].*

## Why businesses train and develop employees

Training employees has benefits both for the individual who is being trained and for the business itself. Training is important for the following reasons:

### Motivation

By investing in training a member of staff, a business is giving that employee the opportunity to learn new skills and develop themselves. This can be extremely motivating for an employee as they may feel valued by the business. As a result, the employee will be happier, which can lead to greater productivity or providing better customer service.

### Retention

Employees will feel that the business really cares about them if they are allowed to learn new skills through training facilitated by the business. This will make the employees more loyal and committed to the business. As a result, they are less likely to leave, improving the business' employee retention rate. Businesses have to be aware that upskilling employees could result in them leaving to get a higher paid job with another firm.

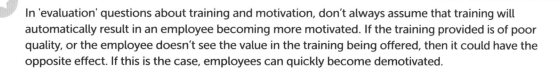

In 'evaluation' questions about training and motivation, don't always assume that training will automatically result in an employee becoming more motivated. If the training provided is of poor quality, or the employee doesn't see the value in the training being offered, then it could have the opposite effect. If this is the case, employees can quickly become demotivated.

### Training and technology

Technology has revolutionised how training is delivered. Webinars and online courses have made self-learning much more accessible. It has also allowed employees to access courses remotely that they may not have been able to attend in the past. This provides a cost saving to the business as they no longer have to pay for employees to travel to attend formal courses.

Technology has also changed the type and format of training. Using simulations in medical, dentistry and aviation professions, for example, allows employees to train without the pressure and consequences of things going wrong.

2. Explain **one** impact on a business' workforce when new technology is introduced. [3]

*Whenever new technology is introduced, a business will have to re-train employees to be able to use it.[1] This means that the business will incur extra costs on top of the cost of purchasing the technology[1]. In the short-term this could make the business less profitable[1].*

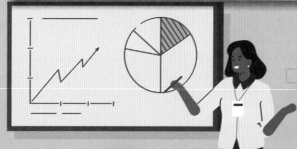

# MOTIVATION

Motivation can be defined as the reason an employee acts or behaves in a certain way. It is their desire or willingness to complete a task. To be successful, a business needs motivated staff who can be enthused or encouraged using financial or non-financial methods.

## The importance of motivation in the workplace

**Motivation** is important for a number of reasons:

- It helps with **retention** by keeping **staff turnover** low. Staff turnover is the percentage of the workforce who leave over a period of time.
- It can help to lower staff absence rates as employees enjoy coming to work.
- It helps to attract new employees. People will want to come and work for a business that looks after them.
- It can lead to employees providing better customer service, enhancing a business' reputation.
- It can lead to a more committed workforce who want to be involved in helping the business succeed. As a result they may be more likely to provide new ideas.
- It can help to improve communication within a business.
- It can lead to an increase in **productivity** for a business.

1. Explain **one** benefit to a business of having motivated employees. [3]

*If employees are motivated, they are likely to be more productive[1]. This is because they are happier and so will work harder to help make the business a success[1]. As a result, the business may become more efficient as products will be made more efficiently, with fewer mistakes[1].*

## Financial methods of motivation

### Remuneration

The term used to describe the pay or financial rewards that are given to an employee in return for their work or services provided.

### Bonus

A sum of money paid to an employee for achieving a target. It can also be paid to staff as a result of the business performing well.

### Commission

This usually forms part of the remuneration package for sales staff. For every sale made, the employee will receive a percentage of that sale in income.

### Fringe benefits

Perks that carry a financial value that are given to employees. They include: private health insurance, a company car, pension schemes, company discounts and free gym membership.

### Promotion

Being rewarded with a job that carries more authority and with it, a higher salary or wage.

## Non-financial methods of motivation

Non-financial methods of motivation are ways that a business can motivate their employees without involving a monetary reward.

### Job rotation

**Job rotation** gives employees opportunities to work in a number of different areas, completing a range of jobs. This is particularly useful where the jobs being completed are low skilled and boring. Giving the worker variety will motivate them as they won't have to do the same repetitive job continuously. This also benefits the business; if an employee is absent then the business will have employees who have the skills and experience to cover them. However, this will only work if the varied jobs a worker completes are not as boring as each other. Simply swapping one boring job for another may not motivate at all.

### Job enrichment

**Job enrichment** is provided by giving an employee tasks that carry greater responsibility.

Job enrichment will work as a motivation tool as long as the employee has the necessary skills to cope with the extra responsibility. If they don't, they may feel stressed and under pressure, which could actually demotivate them.

### Autonomy

Giving employees **autonomy** means empowering them to make decisions about their own working life. This makes employees feel trusted and that their contribution is valued. Therefore, they will be more motivated to work.

2. Explain **one** reason why job enrichment may improve employee motivation. [3]

*Job enrichment will motivate an employee because it gives workers a new challenge[1]. By being given the responsibility to complete this new challenge, workers will feel valued by the business[1]. Therefore, they will feel less bored and more worthwhile.[1]*

Be careful with questions in the exam about motivation. The question above asks you to explain how job enrichment motivates the worker, not what the benefit of having a motivated workforce is to the business. If you answer the question by giving benefits to the business of using job enrichment, rather than explaining why it works as a method of motivation, you would be unlikely to score many marks. Be careful to answer the question being asked.

# CASE STUDY

**GrantTree Ltd is one of the UK's leading innovation funding specialists. They will secure sources of finance for clients who may have a unique idea that they want to bring to market. They help new businesses obtain grants, loans and other forms of financial assistance.**

*GrantTree* were founded back in 2010 by Paulina and Daniel Tenner. They wanted to build a company together that could offer serious support to other start-ups, tech companies, and innovators. In the nine years since, *GrantTree* have gone from strength to strength, growing quickly and have now raised over £100m for their clients.

*GrantTree* have a very unique way in which they organise and motivate their staff. Employees at *GrantTree* have complete autonomy and empowerment over their own working lives. No one is line managed by anyone. They term it as 'Open Culture' which allows staff to have complete flexibility when it comes to how they work. Employees can choose what they do, when to work and where to work. If an employee wakes up in the morning and would prefer to work from home that day, then they can. No one tells them what to do or where to be and staff actually set their own salaries.

There is a flat structure at *GrantTree*. Each employee can make important decisions within their own working life. Although this gives freedom, employees cannot take the traditional promotion route as there is no hierarchical structure. An employee can take on additional responsibility by signing up for more duties as the business practices Holacracy. Holacracy creates one set of rules for everyone and allows anyone to take on a new role or duty within the company. If someone joined as a sales executive or a developer, they could also try working in recruitment or marketing.

# EXAMINATION PRACTICE

1.  Which **one** of the following is a fringe benefit? [1]
    A – Bonus
    B – Commission
    C – Free lunch
    D – Wage

2.  Which **one** of the following is a financial method of motivation? [1]
    A – Autonomy
    B – Job enrichment
    C – Job rotation
    D – Promotion

3.  Explain **one** reason why a business may provide a person specification as part of their recruitment process. [3]

4.  Explain **one** drawback to a business of recruiting internally. [3]

5.  Explain **one** benefit to a business of using informal training. [3]

6.  Discuss the impact to a business of operating a centralised structure. [6]

**For the following questions you must refer to the case study on the previous page.**

7.  Outline **one** reason why training might be important to *GrantTree*. [2]

8.  Outline why effective communication is important to *GrantTree*. [2]

9.  Analyse the impact on *GrantTree* from operating with a flat organisational structure. [6]

10. Analyse the benefit to *GrantTree* from offering its employees flexible working. [6]

11. Evaluate whether allowing employees to select their own salaries is the most effective method for *GrantTree* to motivate its employees.
    You should use the information provided as well as your knowledge of business. [12]

# EXAMINATION PRACTICE ANSWERS

## Section 1.1

1.  D                                                                                                                    [1]

2.  C, D                                                                                                                 [2]

3.  A business may add value by having a better design for their product. This may mean that the product is more aesthetically pleasing than others in the market. As a result, it will grab the attention of customers when they see it on the shelves.

    A business may add value by having a strong brand name. This allows the business to charge more for their products because customers would be willing to pay higher prices in order to obtain branded goods. This may enable the business to generate more profit.

    A unique selling point may also add value. This makes a product different compared to its competitors. This, therefore allows a business to charge more as customers would be willing to pay to get a unique product.                          [3]

4.  An entrepreneur may employ people. People are classed as human resources, who need to be kept happy. By doing this, the entrepreneur will get the best out of their workers. As a result, more work will be completed.                          [3]

5.  By running their own business, an entrepreneur will have independence. This is because the entrepreneur is their own boss and they don't have to answer to anyone else. This allows them freedom to make the decisions they want to.             [3]

6.  Khadija taught dance at a local school. Therefore, she was able to see a gap in the market for this kind of activity for children.  [1]

7.  Khadija faces the risk of running out of cash. This is because she keeps the price of her dance lessons low, therefore, she does not receive a large amount of cash inflows. As a result, she could face the risk of not being able to pay her dance teachers, which may cause them to stop working in the dance school.

    Khadija also risks her security. This is because her dance school may not bring in regular cash inflows. Her income is dependent on a number of people attending her dance lessons. Should they not turn up, the business may not have enough funds to be able to give her a sufficient income, meaning that she may not be able to pay for all her monthly outgoings.           [6]

8.  Khadija will seek a financial reward for taking on the risk of running the dance school. If she can earn more revenue than she has to pay out in costs (such as the wages for her dance teachers), then she will be able to make profit. She could choose to retain the profit and reinvest the money into growing the dance school, by investing in more studios and hiring more teachers so that she can offer more disciplines, such as ballet. This could cause her future sales to grow even more, leading to even more studios and greater profit.

    Profit may not be the main reward that Khadija may seek. Her main reward may be personal satisfaction. She may want the dance school to be successful through her pupils earning awards and medals from performing at local dance shows. This would give her recognition, helping her to develop a good reputation for producing top level dancers. This may lead to more children wanting to join her classes and musical productions.

    Overall, seeing her pupils succeed at shows and being involved in dance will be more important to Khadija than making as much profit as possible. We know that she wants to involve as many people in the community as possible in her shows, so I think that this is her main reason. However, this will depend on the dance school making sufficient revenue to cover costs. Without being financially stable, the dance school would not exist, but personal satisfaction comes before profit.                 [12]

## Section 1.2

1.  B                                                                                                                    [1]

2.  A                                                                                                                    [1]

3.  A focus group provides detailed feedback from potential customers. This will allow them to make the desired alterations in order to ensure the product meets their needs, which could potentially lead to greater sales for the business.            [3]

4.  A business can more easily collect large amounts of quantitative data. This is because it is expressed in numerical form, allowing the business to show data on a chart or graph, which can then be more easily analysed.                          [3]

5.  One drawback is that the data might be out of date. This is because it has been collected by someone else at a previous point in time. As a result, a business may make a bad decision based on inaccurate data.                                 [3]

6.  He could offer garden waste removal / planting / pruning services. (There are many other valid responses.)                  [1]

7.  Micah could segment the market by age. As he found out, Chedgrave has a high proportion of elderly people, so he can tailor his services to this age category.                                                                              [2]

8.  One impact is that Micah will have to monitor the services of the other gardening and landscaping businesses to see what they are offering. This is so he can differentiate his gardening service by utilising his expertise in horticulture. If he just offers the same

mowing and gardening service as other landscapers, then he will not attract enough customers. As a result his sales will be low, which may mean that he doesn't receive sufficient revenue to breakeven.

Another impact is that he may have to charge his customers a lower price for his gardening services. This is because if he is not competitively priced, he may lose out to rivals such as Green Gardens Ltd. This will mean that his margins on each garden job completed will be lower, therefore having to have to attract more people wanting work done in their garden to breakeven.  [6]

9.  Micah's research on the Internet was effective because it allowed him to find out who his major competitors were, including Green Gardens Ltd. As a result of this, he was able to create a market map. This revealed a gap in the market for an upmarket gardening service. Knowing this may enable him to meet the needs of these customers and therefore gain sufficient sales to make his business a success. Without this research, he may not have been able to do this.

It can be argued that his market research was not effective as he only surveyed his friends and family. His friends and family would more than likely tell him what he wants to hear. Therefore, the information may be biased, as his friends and family would want his gardening business to be successful. As a result, he may think it was a positive idea but actually there may not be enough customers wanting help with the design and upkeep of their gardens for it to be successful and Micah may have already invested in it.

Overall, although had it had flaws, his research was effective. The main reason is that his business is more than likely going to start off as a small operation. He did find that his main competitor was Green Gardens Ltd which helped him to spot a gap in the market. However, whether it was very effective will depend on how representative his friends and family are of his target market. If this sample was large and would use Micah for their gardening needs, then it is likely to be more effective. If they are not, then he could be making decisions on unreliable data.  [12]

## Section 1.3

1.  C  [1]

2.  A, B  [2]

3.  An entrepreneur will have a large amount of start-up costs that they will need to pay. As a result, cash outflows will be high and as they are new and unestablished, their receipts will be low. This may cause negative cash flow, therefore focusing on survival is important.  [3]

4.  A business will need cash to pay its employees. Without paying them, they would very quickly stop working for the business. As a result, the business would not be able to produce products or provide a service.  [3]

5.  Breakeven = Fixed costs ÷ (selling price − variable cost per unit)
    5,000 ÷ 200 = 25. 2,000 ÷ 200 = 10. 25 − 10 = 15 units.  [2]

6.  To increase market share, as he is proud to be market leader in the artisan bakery market.  [1]

7.  Profit = revenue − total costs
    Revenue = 1,300 × £1.65 = £2,145
    Total costs = £1,250 + (£0.40 × 1,300) = £1,770
    Profit = £2,145 - £1,770 = £375.  [2]

8.  Margin of safety = actual output − break even level of output
    Margin of safety = 1,300 − 1,000 = 300 units.  [2]

9.  Robert should use a bank loan. One reason for this is that the bakery can get all the money it needs for the van immediately. This would allow the bakery to start delivering goods to more outlets in Wiltshire and Somerset more quickly. This would mean that sales of the breads and cakes will increase sooner, allowing the bakery to increase its revenue sooner than if they had to save up their profit.

A drawback of using the bank loan is that it could be expensive compared to using retained profit. This is because the bank will charge interest on top. This means that the fixed costs of the bakery will increase. As a result, Gibbs Bakery will need to sell more than the 1,000 breads and cakes to breakeven. Therefore, by borrowing the money to purchase the vans, the risk of failure for the bakery is increased.

Overall, I believe that they should borrow the money from the bank rather than using retained profit. This is because the business needs to meet the needs of its customers quickly. By obtaining the full amount of finance straight away the bakery can buy the vans more quickly and start delivering its breads and cakes to the retail outlets sooner, thus increasing revenues. However, this will depend on the rate of interest charged. If the interest charged is too high, then the extra revenue raised may be offset by the increase in costs and make the investment not worthwhile.  [9]

10.  One way that Gibbs Bakery can increase profits is to increase the price they charge for their breads and cakes. They are known for selling high quality baked goods so customers may be willing to pay more. This may lead to increased revenue (if sales don't fall as a result) which could potentially lead to increased profits.

An alternative way to increase profits is to decrease costs. The bakery could do this by using cheaper ingredients for its breads and cakes, by finding a cheaper supplier of flour and yeast for example. This would lower the bakery's variable costs overall from the current level of £0.40 per unit. As a result, total costs will fall, increasing profits, as long as sales remained the same.

Overall, the bakery should increase the price. The main reason being that they are known for selling top quality breads and confections. This excellent reputation allows them to charge more and gives the image that they are a high-class bakery. If they used cheaper supplies, it may affect the quality and then lower this reputation. However, increasing the price is dependent on how the increase in price is perceived. If they lose a lot of customers as a result, then it may not be the best option. If the customers perceive the bread and cakes to be worth paying a higher price for, then it will certainly be the most effective way to increase profits. [12]

## Section 1.4

1. C [1]

2. C, D [2]

3. One benefit is that the franchisor may conduct promotion. This means that the franchisee does not need to pay for expensive marketing costs. This will help to keep the total costs low, therefore reducing the break-even level of output. [3]

4. If a business locates away from a competitor, it may reduce the amount of competition that a business faces in a certain area. This means that if customers want the product or service, they will have to buy from that business. This could lead to increased revenues than if they located near their rivals. [3]

5. One reason is that it gives customers greater choice of models to select from. This will make them more likely to purchase from Woodkit. [2]

6. Technology has had a big impact on the promotion of the business by using digital communications. Woodkit sends out an e-newsletter to regular customers promoting the special offers they have on models and accessories. [2]

7. Being a limited company means that the Graham and his family will have limited liability. This reduces the risk that they face in running their modelling company. This is because they are seen as separate legal entities from the business. This means that if the sales of models and accessories fall, meaning the business cannot afford to pay for the debts that it has, Graham and his family will not have to sell their personal possessions to pay for it.

   Another impact is that it may be easier to grow their modelling business. This is because it is easier to raise finance. They can sell shares in the company to other investors interested in the modelling market. This could increase the cash flowing into the business, so the business could extend its operations in other countries which they already sell to, such as Australia and the USA. [6]

8. One benefit is that it would help Graham see the risks involved, particularly in selling abroad. Part of his plan would have been to sell to modelling enthusiasts in the USA and Australia. Before doing so, he would have looked at, and planned for, the risks involved in trading with customers abroad; therefore when circumstances arise, he would be able to deal with them.

   A second benefit is that he would have been able to use the business plan to help raise finance. Woodkit stock a large product range and to get all the models and accessories from all the other brands would have cost a lot of money to begin with. By forecasting his finances, Graham would have been able to prove to investors that there would be sufficient demand for his models and accessories to have enough cash flowing into the business to cover any repayments needed. This would have helped to reduce the risk of taking on finance that couldn't be paid back. [6]

9. Product may be the most important element of the marketing mix to the business. A large number of their customers are enthusiastic collectors of models and accessories, so will have specific needs. The models and accessories that the business sells must be of the make and quality that the collectors expect. If they are not, then they will likely purchase the models from another firm. This would mean that sales would be low, potentially harming revenues and causing the firm not to be able to sell enough models and accessories to breakeven.

   However, it could be argued that place is the most important factor. Woodkit has decided to locate purely on the Internet rather than having a physical store. This has allowed them to reach the American and Australian markets. This has allowed sales of models and accessories to be higher than they would have been, meaning that revenue and profit have been higher than if they had chosen a physical location.

   Overall, the product is probably the most important factor. This is because they are selling products that collectors want. If they didn't stock the right models and accessories, customers wouldn't purchase from them. However, just having the right products alone wouldn't make the business a success. They need to have an integrated marketing mix. The products need to be right and collectors need to know the models and accessories that are available. They need to be sensibly priced and being on the Internet allows the business to maximise sales. [12]

## Section 1.5

1. D [1]

2. A [1]

3. New technology can allow a business to cut their costs. This is because workers could be replaced by machinery and robots. This would allow a business to cut the wage bill. This will lower total costs, which may make them more competitive. [3]

4. By complying with consumer law, a business will gain a good reputation. As a result, customers may become loyal and repeat purchase. This would potentially lead to increased sales and revenue for the business. [3]

5. Rising inflation may mean that the cost of supplies increases. This will cause a business' variable costs to increase which may mean that it is passed onto customers in the form of increased prices. This may cause sales to decrease. [3]

6. One impact is that repayments on loans from banks will be lower. This will lower a business' fixed costs. As a result, total costs will be lower, which will mean that it is easier for a business to breakeven, increasing its chances of success.

   A second impact is that consumers will now have more disposable income. This is because they will be paying less for any personal loans they have. As a result, demand in an economy may rise, potentially increasing a business' sales. As a result, revenues may increase which could possibly lead to the business making more profit. [6]

7. £110 × 1.2 = €132. [2]

8. If the pound were to fall in value against the Euro, then the hotel might receive more guests from Europe. This is because it would now be cheaper for foreign tourists to visit the UK. [2]

9. The hotel will have a positive impact on the local community. The hotel attracts tourists to the area because they choose to stay at the hotel. These tourists will then spend time out and about in the local town where the hotel is situated. In doing so, they will spend money with other businesses. This therefore increases the income of other businesses in the local area, providing them with a greater source of income.

   They may have a negative impact as the hotel could indirectly contribute to traffic, noise and light pollution in the area, upsetting local residents. This is exacerbated as the hotel is on the river and attracts lots of tourists on boating holidays. The fuel from the deliveries and boats may cause pollution and the noise of the engines may disturb wildlife. This could upset more of the community as they will not benefit from wildlife that may move away as a direct result. [6]

10. Technology has allowed the hotel to improve its communication with customers. This is because they can now take advantage of social media platforms like Facebook and Twitter. This allows them to showcase, very quickly and cheaply, what events the hotel is offering such as themed nights in the restaurant. As they can do this for free, their costs will be kept low, allowing them to competitively price their hotel rooms and food served in the restaurant.

    Another impact is that it has allowed them to increase the number of potential tourists that they can attract. Through their website and by being on travel sites such as booking.com, tourists form Europe can now easily find out about the hotel and book a stay with them. If e-commerce didn't exist, it would have been harder and less likely for these tourists to find this hotel. This means that the hotels sales are higher than they would have been, increasing the hotel's chance of selling all the rooms and therefore being successful. [6]

11. The state of the economy may be the biggest external influence on the business. This is because if economic activity falls, consumers will have less disposable income. If this is the case, then there will be less demand for hotel rooms and fewer people choosing to eat out in restaurants. This is because these are seen as luxury purchases and if people have less income, they will cut this expenditure first. This will cause fewer people to visit the hotel and restaurant, meaning that the business may struggle to breakeven.

    On the other hand, legislation has a big influence on the hotel. This is because the hotel will have to follow strict health and safety guidance for the benefit of guests and employees. For example, the kitchen will have strict legislation placed on it in terms of cleanliness and hygiene. Ensuring that the kitchen, and other areas of the hotel, meet these regulations can incur additional expenditure, which increases total costs to the hotel causing them to become less competitive.

    Overall, all external factors will have a big influence at some point, and they cannot always be foreseen. However, the main thing is that the hotel and restaurant are seen as luxury expenditure and will be one of the first things to go should consumers' disposable income drop sharply; therefore this may have the biggest impact. However, it depends on the costs of ensuring they meet regulations as these can be passed onto the consumer as long as it doesn't make them too uncompetitive. [12]

## Section 2.1

1. C [1]

2. B [1]

3. A business may have to change its objectives because economic activity decreases / a major competitor enters the market. [1]

4. One drawback of growing via a takeover is that it is risky. This is because it is hard to make two businesses work as one. This happens if the employees of the business that is taken over dislike like the management style, aims or vision of the new business and therefore may be demotivated. [3]

5. One drawback of selling assets to raise capital is that there may be a limit on how much can be raised. This is because a business needs assets to produce products and provide services, so can only sell the ones that are no longer used. As a result, they may not have enough to finance their intended growth and will need to use other sources as well. [3]

6. One impact of globalisation is that a business now faces more competition. This is because customers can now more easily import rival products from foreign businesses. This may mean that it is harder for a domestic business to make enough sales to breakeven. [3]

7. One impact of becoming a plc is that a business is able to raise more finance. This is because they can sell shares to the general public on the stock exchange. This would give them a large amount of extra capital to help grow the business, which may mean that the business can increase its sales.

   Another impact is that they are more at risk from a takeover. This is because the shares are now able to be bought by the general public and other businesses. If an individual or business bought over 50% of the shares, they would have a controlling interest, meaning that the original owners would no longer have control. [6]

8. One benefit is that it makes the food and clothes that M&S sell more competitively priced compared to overseas competitors. This is because foreign imports will be charged a tax, making them more expensive. [2]

9. One method they use is to adapt their products to fit the market, for instance they could 'localise' their food products to fit the local culture. This would make their products more attractive to the local population. [2]

10. They should use retained profit. The main advantage that retained profit has over share capital is that it allows the current ownership not to be diluted. This means that if the shareholders like the ethical and environmentally friendly approach that the managers have taken through the implementation of Plan A, they will allow them to continue. Should new shareholders come in and dislike this approach, they could potentially vote the management out and take the business in a new direction, which may mean that the business is not as ethically focused.

    However, the multinational retailer may not be able to raise sufficient funds by using retained profit. M&S have seen a fall in profit before tax of 20.2% recently. This means that they have not been making as much profit and may not have sufficient funds to invest in opening up new stores in foreign countries. As a result, they may have to seek alternative finance anyway.

    Overall, retained profit would be the best source. The key for M&S is in keeping their ethical and environmentally friendly approach. Without this, they would lose their USP. If they issued shares, it could potentially put this at risk if the current shareholders became outnumbered. However, this is dependent on the amount of finance needed. If it is more than they have in profits, which may be the case with their falling profits, then M&S will need to use a different source, regardless. [9]

11. The ethical approach that M&S have taken is the correct one because consumers are becoming increasingly ethically minded when buying food and clothes. They want food that has come from local sources and is Fairtrade. They also want clothes that have been ethically manufactured. By providing this, M&S have been recognised and have received awards from organisations such as The Climate Change Coalition. This gives the retailer a good reputation, meaning that consumers are more likely to purchase from them, potentially increasing revenues and profits.

    However, it could be argued that this is the wrong strategy to focus on. This is because by being ethical, it can cause additional expenditure. For instance, by paying the suppliers more than the minimum wage, it increases total costs, causing profits to fall. Falling profits is something that M&S have experienced as can be seen by the fall in profit before tax of 20.2% between March 2019 and March 2020. This would make shareholders unhappy as the return on their investment is lowered.

    In conclusion, it is the right thing to do morally. M&S have been recognised for their work and the ongoing reputational benefits may help to improve profits longer term as ethics and the environment become more of a prominent issue. Also, the key here is that although profits fell, the retailer still made £67.2m profit before tax. If they wanted to reverse the fall in profits, perhaps the management could look at cost savings in areas that won't have a negative impact on stakeholders or the environment. [12]

## Section 2.2

1. A [1]

2. D [1]

3. Knowing which stage of the life cycle a product is in allows a business to know how much and what kind of promotion is needed. For instance, when in growth, they can ensure that promotion is centred around raising further awareness of the product, so more people know it is available. When the product is in decline, they can focus on using sales promotion techniques in order to slow the decline. This can improve sales. [3]

4. A business may use a high price strategy because they have added a lot of value in the production process. This could lead to the business having a superior product in terms of functionality. As a result, customers may feel that it is worth spending more money on it. [3]

5. The brand may gain a lot of exposure, particularly if they sponsor a high-profile event. As a result, more customers may become aware of the brand and want to be associated with the brand. This could encourage customers to purchase products and services from the business, leading to an increase in sales. This may result in an increase in revenue and could potentially lead to an increase in profits, as long as the cost of sponsorship does not outweigh the increase in revenue. [6]

6. ASOS differentiates its clothing range by offering a large variety of different sizes (30 different sizes). This means that they have a wider product range compared to other rivals so are more likely to be able to meet customer needs. [2]

7. ASOS could extend the life cycle of its clothing range by offering items at a discount. For example, they could offer summer wear at discounted prices when the summer is over, encouraging more people to purchase. [2]

8. The design mix is important because the clothes have to function. For example, customers would not expect a dress to tear easily. If it did, then customers would be unhappy with the quality. As a result, they would be less likely to shop with the clothes retailer again, perhaps choosing a rival, such as Next, instead. This could lead to a poor reputation, leading to fewer sales.

As a retailer of fashion, the appearance of the clothes is particularly important to ASOS. The clothes need to be eye-catching to the consumer. If they are, then ASOS is more likely to be successful in selling the garment. If a customer finds an item appealing, they may picture themselves wearing it on social media, which will help to make more people aware of it and consequently a positive reputation will be developed as a result. [6]

9. The competitive nature of the market will influence ASOS's pricing strategy. ASOS is operating in a very competitive market against major retailers such as Next, boohoo and PrettyLittleThing. As there is a lot of choice for customers, it means that ASOS may have to keep their prices low, otherwise they may lose business. If they are more expensively priced, the business may not make enough sales to cover costs, which could cause cash flow difficulties for the firm.

The life cycle of the clothing will also have an influence. As new fashionable items are launched, they may be able to charge more for the clothing as people will want to buy the latest fashions. As these fashions change and the items start to become obsolete, the business may have to lower the price to encourage customers to purchase end-of-line clothing. [6]

10. Promotion has been a huge source of competitive advantage for ASOS through its uses of digital marketing. They have had many promotional campaigns like the #AsSeenOnMe Instagram stories campaign. This clearly engaged customers as more than 3 million interacted with it. This, and their other campaigns, have given them great advantage over competitors as their success shows. This means that the brand has had great exposure, which has probably contributed to the 2.3 billion visits to their platforms, potentially meaning that the business sells more and therefore may have made more profit as a result.

However, you could argue that the product and service that the business provides gives them a greater advantage than the promotion. Their recent trial allowing shoppers to see what the item of clothing looks like on different sized models is very innovative and unique compared to other online fashion retailers. This differentiating factor may be the reason why shoppers have chosen to use ASOS over rivals, leading to higher sales.

Overall, their promotion is giving them a competitive advantage as without these viral social media campaigns shoppers may not visit them in the first place. However, it cannot be the only source of advantage in such a competitive market. When the shoppers are attracted to the website through the social media campaigns, there must also be something there that differentiates them from rivals and gives the customers a reason to buy from them. To be successful the fashion retailer has used various strategies to give them competitive advantage and must continue to do so. [12]

## Section 2.3

1. D [1]

2a. Size of order A = 200 units (250 units − 50 units). [2]

2b. Lead time of order B = 15 days (25 days − 10 days). [2]

3. One benefit is that the business can charge a high price for the product. This is because the product will be manufactured to meet the exact requirements of each individual customer. Therefore, the business may receive a large profit margin on the sale of each product. [3]

4. One benefit is that the business will be able to meet large one-off orders. This is because they will have plenty of stock on hand to cover the increase in demand. This will lead to the customers' needs being met more quickly and therefore they will be satisfied, giving the business a good reputation. [3]

5. One benefit is that staff can answer all questions that customers may have. As a result, customers will be pleased with the service they have received. This may mean that customers are more likely to return. [3]

6. One benefit of automation is that Toyota has become more productive as it is now able to produce cars more quickly. Therefore, they have been able to reduce the average cost of making each vehicle. [2]

7. It is important that Toyota choose the right supplier so that they get good quality materials when they need them. Toyota cars, such as the Corolla, have a reputation for high quality and therefore the materials used must not compromise this. [2]

8. One impact is that each individual car is going to be manufactured to the exact, same specifications. Therefore, the quality of the cars will be consistent. This has helped to give the vehicle manufacturer a reputation for quality and as a result, customers will continue to buy cars such as the Corolla.

Another impact is that the average cost of producing each vehicle is reduced. This will mean that Toyota can reduce the price of its cars. This leads to them becoming more price competitive with rivals such as Volkswagen and Hyundai. This could cause more motorists to purchase a Toyota, which has contributed to nearly 9 million sales last year. [6]

9. One impact is that waste is minimised. This is because the materials needed to manufacture a car are only ordered when needed. This means that when a model of car becomes obsolete, Toyota will not be left with lots of car parts that they no longer require. This increases efficiency for the vehicle manufacturer, leading to a reduced average cost of production.

Another impact is that they may run out of car components. This could happen due to a delay in delivery from the supplier. This would lead to a production of the vehicles being halted. As a result, delivery to customers may be delayed, which will have a negative impact on their reputation, giving General Motors and other rivals an advantage. [6]

10. Toyota's quality assurance programme has given it an advantage as it ensures that there are minimal defects. The quality of the cars is checked at each stage of the production process. This means that the business will have reduced waste. This helps to keep the average cost of producing each vehicle down to a minimum, allowing their cars, such as the Corolla, to be competitively priced.

However, it can be argued that it is not the quality assurance system that gives the vehicle manufacturer its advantage. But it is the fact that the car's functionality is superior to that of rival manufacturers such as Hyundai. One of the reasons that over 43 million Corollas have been sold over the years is the fact that they function well and last a long time. This gives motorists a reason to purchase a Toyota car over rival vehicles.

In conclusion, the durability of the car is a key selling point and one that definitely gives the vehicle manufacturer its competitive advantage. This is an important factor in a motorist's decision to purchase a new car as they don't want to have to keep getting their car repaired. The functionality of the car, may however, be dependent on the thoroughness of the quality checks that take place. Without having the quality assurance system, errors may go undetected and the business may lose its reputation for quality and reliability. [12]

## Section 2.4

1. C [1]

2. C [1]

3. A business could improve its gross profit by reducing its costs of sales. This could be done by finding a different supplier. This could lower the cost of buying the raw materials used in the production of the product. This could lead to increased profit margin per product and therefore, if sales remain constant, gross profit will increase. (Accept price increase.) [3]

4. A business could use marketing data by finding out what customers think of a product. If they discovered that there was something they disliked, they could then adapt the product. This would mean that the product would become more appealing to customers. [3]

5. One limitation is that data could be historical. This will mean that the business is making decisions about the future based on what has happened in the past. This may mean that the business data is irrelevant and cause the business to make a wrong decision, which could lead to the business getting into financial difficulty.

Another limitation is that statistical data can be easily manipulated. For instance, a manager may make predicted sales figures look better than they are as they may gain, personally, as a result of the business continuing the product line. Therefore, the business may produce products to meet this predicted demand and if it does not materialise, then the business will have a lot of stock left over. This could mean that the business suffers poor cash flow as a result. [6]

6. $(7,500 \div 55,500) \times 100 = 13.51\%$ [2]

7. $133,412 - (24,367) = £157,779$ [2]

8. $(133,412 \div 326,303) \times 100 = 40.89\%$ [2]

9. $(24,820 \div 293,589) \times 100 = 8.45\%$ [2]

10. Wagamama could use their past sales records to prove their financial stability in order to get a loan to finance the opening of more Mamago restaurants. This may help give the bank confidence that Wagamama will be able to make the repayments. [2]

11. They could use the data to help inform what dishes to sell. This is because it tells them that 38% of customers are most satisfied by the healthy dishes Wagamama sells. Therefore, this could inform the management that they should continue to produce a wide variety of healthy meals as it helps them to stand out from others such as Nando's and Pizza Express.

They could also use it to see that their speed of service may be an area that they need to improve on. This is because in the research, more customers are satisfied with Nando's speed of service compared to Wagamama's. Therefore, to improve customer satisfaction, Wagamama could adapt its operations in order to get meals out more quickly. [6]

12. Opening more Mamago restaurants may be the best way to increase profit as there is a growing demand for food on the go. As a result, if there are more Mamago outlets then more customers will be able to purchase dishes like the katsu chicken salad. This could lead to increased revenue and potentially may increase the profits of the business.

Alternatively, it may not be the best way to improve the profitability as sales is not the issue for the restaurant chain. From the accounts, we can see that revenue has increased over the year, but they moved from a profit in 2018 to a loss in 2019. This was due to the increase in expenses. If Wagamama can cut these indirect costs, then overall net profit may increase leading to greater profitability.

In conclusion, the main problem for Wagamama is that expenses have increased hugely and therefore need addressing in order to increase the profitability. The restaurant must look deeper at this issue and see what caused the increase and then decide how best to rectify it. However, this does not mean that they should scrap the opening of new Mamago restaurants. To improve profits, a business can increase revenue or cut costs. Therefore, a combination of cutting costs and opening new Mamago restaurants could be beneficial, as long as the cost of opening the restaurants does not outweigh the increase in revenue. [12]

1. C [1]

2. D [1]

3. One benefit is that the business and applicants will know and understand the qualifications required of a new position. This means that only people with that relevant qualification will apply. This increases the likelihood of suitable applicants for the job, meaning that time is not wasted. [3]

4. One drawback of recruiting internally is that the business will not get an influx of new ideas. This might mean that the business misses out on opportunities to become more efficient or to do things differently. This means that the business may lose out on potential profit. [3]

5. One benefit is that the employee will still be doing their job whilst they undertake the training. This means that the business continues to be productive and as a result, the business will continue to make sales. [3]

6. One impact is that the senior managers become very powerful as they hold all the authority to make the decisions. This could be problematic if the business is nationwide, because the senior managers may lack understanding of a branch's local market. As a result, they may make a decision that is detrimental to the customers in a certain area and that could cause sales of that particular branch to drop dramatically.

   Another impact is that communication can be slower. This is because the senior managers are the ones who hold the decision-making powers. As a result, it can take time for their decision to filter down to through to the employees, in different regions or departments, lower down the hierarchy. Therefore, the business may be slower to react to any changes in the market. [6]

7. Training might be important as it gives employees different skills. This could be important as they are able to work in different departments. Through Holacracy, they can take on jobs with more responsibility which they will need new skills to complete. [2]

8. Effective communication is important as employees need to fully understand the needs of their clients in order to work out the best way to finance their business idea. This will then allow the employee to be more successful in gaining the finance the client needs. [2]

9. One impact from operating a flat organisational structure is that there is more empowerment given to employees. This is because no one has a line manager. Each employee is responsible for their own working lives as there is no one supervising them. For instance, employees can choose when and where they work. This means that the business must recruit employees that can cope with working in this way, otherwise the business may have employees who do not work as hard as they might, were they constantly supervised. If this was the case, then the business would be much less productive. [6]

10. One impact of allowing employees to have complete flexibility in terms of their working life means that the business can attract a high-quality calibre of employee. People will want to work in a business that trusts their employees as GrantTree do. The fact that an employee can get up in the morning and choose to work from home, or work form anywhere, is appealing. This means that when they need to recruit employees, they will not struggle to get the quality applicants they are looking for.

    Another impact is that allowing employees flexible working practices can be motivating. Allowing the employees to choose the hours they work shows that the business has trust in their employees. As a result, the employees will be more committed to the business. This will make them more determined to ensure they obtain the funding for their client. This could be a reason why the business has been successful and has led to them earning over £100m in government funding for their clients. [6]

11. Allowing employees to select their own salaries is a great way to motivate workers. By allowing them to do so, the funding specialists are showing trust in employees. This allows them to feel valued by the funding company. They feel valued because they can negotiate the amount of pay that they feel that they are worth. They will feel happy with how the business treats them. As a result, the workers will be more inclined to ensure that the business' clients get the funding that they need, therefore showing that they are motivated to do a good job.

    Alternatively, it could be argued that the system of combined job enrichment and job rotation that GrantTree employ is better at motivating the workers. Allowing workers to sign up for extra responsibilities in different departments provides variety. This variety will ensure that boredom does set in, as someone who was employed to work in sales can also choose to contribute in other areas, such as recruitment.

    In conclusion, the key motivating factor in this business is trust. The owners of GrantTree trust employees to do the right thing with regards to their salary. It is likely that someone who would simply choose to pay themselves an astronomical amount, would probably not be hired in the first place. All the factors that they have put in place will help them to motivate staff and therefore maximise the funding that they gain for clients. However, all these measures depend on the individual. The individual has to have the right characteristics, otherwise these measures wouldn't motivate them. [12]

# LEVELS BASED MARK SCHEME FOR EXTENDED RESPONSE QUESTIONS

Questions that require extended writing use mark bands. The whole answer will be marked together to determine which mark band it fits into and which mark should be awarded within the mark band.

| Discuss | Analysis | Justify | Evaluate | |
|---------|----------|---------|----------|---|
| 5–6 marks | 5–6 marks | 7–9 marks | 9–12 marks | Response demonstrates accurate knowledge and understanding of business concepts and issues throughout, including appropriate use of business terminology (AO1b). Knowledge and understanding of business concepts and issues is applied, in detail, to the business context throughout (AO2). Business information and/or issues are deconstructed, finding detailed interconnected points with logical chains of reasoning (AO3a). Response draws a valid and well-reasoned conclusion based on a thorough evaluation of business information and issues (AO3b). |
| 3–4 marks | 3–4 marks | 4–6 marks | 5–8 marks | Response demonstrates mostly accurate knowledge and understanding of business concepts and issues, including appropriate use of business terminology in places (AO1b). Knowledge and understanding of business concepts and issues are applied to the business context, although there may be some inconsistencies (AO2). Response shows deconstruction of business information and/or issues, finding interconnected points with chains of reasoning, although there may be some logical inconsistencies (AO3a). Response draws a conclusion based on sound evaluation of business information and issues (AO3b). |
| 1–2 marks | 1–2 marks | 1–3 marks | 1–4 marks | Response demonstrates elements of knowledge and understanding of business concepts and issues, with limited business terminology used (AO1b). Limited application of knowledge and understanding of business concepts to the business context (AO2). Response attempts to deconstruct business information and/or issues, finding limited connections between points (AO3a). Response draws a conclusion, supported by generic assertions from a limited evaluation of business information and issues (AO3b). |
| 0 marks | 0 marks | 0 marks | 0 marks | Response is missing or not worthy of credit. |

**Discuss** questions – **purple** and **green** assessment objectives.
**Analyse** questions – blue and **green** assessment objectives.
**Justify** questions – blue, **green** and **red** assessment objectives.
**Evaluation** questions – **all** assessment objectives.

# INDEX

## H

health and safety  36
hierarchical structure  72
human resources  5

## I

ideas  2
imports  47
incorporation  27
inflation  39
inorganic growth  44
insolvency  22
interest  24
interest rates  19, 39
internal growth  44
international trade  48
Internet  11, 48

## J

jargon  73
job
  description  75
  enrichment  79
  production  60
  rotation  79
just in time (JIT)  62

## L

lead time  61
legislation  36, 46
  changes in...  40
liability  27
  limited  27
loan capital  45
location  12, 14, 29, 47

## M

margin of safety  21
margins  67
mark allocations  vi
market
  conditions  46
  data  69
  map  13
  narrowing  12
  research  9, 10
  segments  54
  segmentation  12

marketing
  data  69
  mix  30, 44, 57
Marks & Spencer (M&S)  50
maturity  53
merger  44
motivation  78
multinationals  47

## N

narrowing the market  12
narrow span of control  72
net cash flow  23
net profit  67
non-financial aims  17

## O

objectives  17, 46
obsolete  2
offers  55
ongoing training  76
opening balance  23
operating expenses  67
operational staff  75
operations  60
organic growth  44
organisational structure  72
original ideas  2
overdraft  24
overseas markets  44
ownership  27

## P

partnership  27
part-time contract  74
performance reviews  76
permanent contract  74
person specification  75
place  30, 48, 56
pressure groups  34, 49
price  4, 8, 14, 30, 48, 54
  penetration  54
  skimming  54
primary research  10
private limited company (ltd)  27
procurement  62
product  30, 48, 52
  miles  49
  range  14
  trials  55

production  60
productivity  78
product life cycle  53, 54
professional development  76
profit  3, 18, 21, 67
  retained  24
promotion  30, 48, 55
proximity (location)  29
public limited company  45
purchasing power  39

## Q

qualitative data  11
quality  8, 14
  assurance  63
  control  63
quantitative data  11, 69
questionnaire  10

## R

recruitment  75
remuneration  78
renewable energy  49
re-order level  61
repayment  19
reports  11
research and development  44
retailer  56
retained profit  24, 45
retention  78
retrieval practice  iii
revenue  18
reward  3
risk  3, 5, 31
royalty  28

## S

sales  64
savings  24
secondary research  11
security
  financial  17
  lack of...  3
segmentation  12
senior managers  75
share capital  24, 45
shareholders  27, 34
social media  11, 35, 55
sole trader  27
special offers  55

# FORMULAE

**Revenue** = Selling price × Number of units sold

**Total variable costs** = Variable cost per unit × Number of units sold

**Total costs** = Fixed costs + Variable costs

**Profit** = Revenue − Total costs

**Interest** = (Total repayment − Borrowed amount) ÷ Borrowed amount × 100

**Break even** = Fixed costs ÷ (Selling price − Variable cost per unit)

**Margin of safety** = Actual output − Break even output

**Net cash flow** = Total receipts − Total payments

**Closing balance** = Opening balance + Net cash flow

**Lead time** = Delivery date − Date stock re-ordered

**Gross profit** = Revenue − Cost of sales

**Net profit** = Gross profit − Other operating expenses and interest

**Gross profit margin** = (Gross profit ÷ Revenue) × 100

**Net profit margin** = (Net profit ÷ Revenue) × 100

**ARR** = (Average annual profit ÷ cost of investment) × 100

**Percentage change** = (Difference in figures ÷ Original figure) × 100

**Average** = Total of all the individual values ÷ The number of values in the set

You may have to demonstrate your basic quantitative skills as well as potentially being asked to use business calculations. This could include calculating the percentage change between two figures or calculating the average of a set of data.

# EXAMINATION TIPS

With your examination practice, apply a boundary approximation using the following table. Be aware that boundaries are usually a few percentage points either side of this. (These figures have been taken from the 2019 examination series.)

| Grade | 9 | 8 | 7 | 6 | 5 | 4 | 3 | 2 | 1 |
|---|---|---|---|---|---|---|---|---|---|
| Boundary | 75% | 70% | 64% | 57% | 50% | 43% | 32% | 21% | 10% |

1. Read each question carefully as some students give answers to questions they think are appearing rather than the actual question.

2. In calculation questions, one mark may be awarded for workings out if the final answer is incorrect. Make sure to show your working in case you make a mistake and the answer is incorrect. Workings also help you check through your own answers more quickly at the end of an exam.

3. Calculation questions total eight marks on each paper; make sure you have learned the formulae.

4. Try to not repeat the question in the first line of your response. It will not score you any marks, but simply wastes your time. Avoid losing marks by not finishing the paper.

5. When explaining your points, you need to use clear connectives to show that you are developing the point you have made and not moving onto a separate point. These connectives include; 'thus', 'therefore', 'this means that', 'this leads to', 'because' and 'as a consequence'. This demonstrates your skills of analysis which are assessed in all longer written questions.

6. Ensure that you include the context in 'State' and 'Outline' questions. Many students forget this and throw away easy marks that could be the difference between grades.

7. In 'Justify' questions, you are presented with two options. You do not need to consider both options to score full marks.

8. All questions are marked according to their Assessment Objectives. Each question starts with a command word. Make sure you fully understand what each command word requires you to do. Reading the command verbs at the start of this guide will help you with this.

**Good luck!**

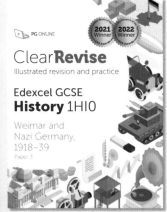
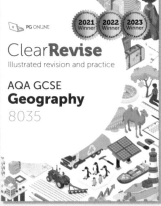

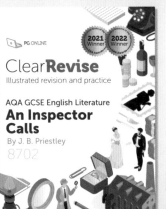
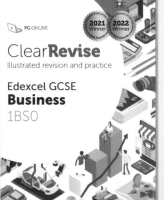